YEOMEN
OF
ENGLAND

Ken Tout

YEOMEN
OF
ENGLAND

TALES OF THE NORTHAMPTONSHIRE YEOMANRY FROM 1794

We remember the humans who died. Spare a
thought too for those superb sentient horses.

First published 2012
By Spellmount, an imprint of

The History Press
The Mill, Brimscombe Port
Stroud, Gloucestershire, GL5 2QG
www.thehistorypress.co.uk

British Library Cataloguing in Publication Data.
A catalogue record for this book is available from the British Library.

ISBN 978 0 7524 6881 5

Typesetting and origination by The History Press
Printed in Great Britain

CONTENTS

NY Association Hon. Secretary, W.J. 'Bill' Hornsey presents a memorial cup to the 2011 army cadet winner. *(Northamptonshire Yeomanry Archives, NYA)*

ACKNOWLEDGEMENTS

T his book was intended originally as a collection of anecdotes from my Second World War regiment, the Northamptonshire Yeomanry. However, a brief survey of history revealed that there are so many fascinating aspects of the Yeomanry and the book seemed to fill up with wider and wider views of a unique formation.

As far as the Northants history is concerned, I appreciated the courtesy of the Chairman of the Regimental Association, Ben Howkins, and also the president, Earl Spencer, in encouraging me to speak freely on the subject according to whatever information I might discover. A main support has been W.J. 'Bill' Hornsey, the indefatigable Hon. Secretary of the Association, who not only has furnished me with contacts and pictures but has himself amassed a wealth of information into which I could dip. We relied much on former members of the regiment who did much research over the years but sadly are no longer with us, including Captain Bill Bellamy, H. de L. Cazenove, George Jelley MBE, Vic Lawrence, Major A.E. 'Sandy' Saunders, Trooper Les 'Spud' Taylor as well as, happily still with us, Captain Tim Deakin, Reg Spittles and Tanky Turner. Many valuable facts and anecdotes were supplied by NY veterans quoted in the text.

Great help and encouragement were offered by Yeomen of the present day, record offices, regimental museums and period enactors. Individual friends who were particularly helpful included Charles, Earl Spencer, Major B. Mollo, Major C. Roads, Captain D. Aiton, Captain J.T. David, Captain A. French, Captain C.A. Parr MBE, Lieutenant Liz Weston, Juliette Baxter, Paul Connell, Geoff Crump, Martin Dawson, Caroline Dwyer, Sarah Elsom, David Fletcher, Jon at Pembroke Museum, Mark Lewis, Paul Robinson, George Streatfeild, and Eleanor Winyard.

It was most enjoyable working with Jo de Vries at The History Press, who is the most helpful and sympathetic of editors, together with her excellent collaborators. A special vote of thanks must go to my wife Jai. The research and writing of this book took place during our removal from Essex to West Sussex and involving the total renovation of our new abode. The author shamelessly quoted press deadlines whilst Jai undertook the marshalling of plumbers, builders and decorators, as well as showing dexterity and versatility with machetes, secateurs, screwdrivers and paint brushes.

FOREWORD
BY EARL SPENCER

The history of the Northamptonshire Yeomanry is distinguished, of course, with consistent bravery in battles fought abroad. But, as the name of the regiment reminds us, this is a local force – and, for me, it is particularly close to home, having so many links with my family, and with Althorp.

George John, 2nd Earl Spencer (my great-great-great grandfather), founded the Yeomanry when Napoleon's France was a terrifying threat to Britain. George John was First Lord of the Admiralty at the time of the Battle of the Nile, and was someone who knew about fighting men: he was arguably Nelson's most prominent patron, giving him what we would term 'fast-track promotion'.

The 5th Earl Spencer also had a record of public service, serving in all of Gladstone's Cabinets, and twice serving as Viceroy of Ireland. It was he who, a little over a century ago, resurrected the Northamptonshire Yeomanry. A Master of the Pytchley, the 'Red Earl' continued the regiment's proud record of producing fine mounts for its men – many of these 'war horses' having learnt their skills pursuing foxes.

My grandfather, Jack – the 7th Earl – was a passionate champion of all things Northamptonshire. Wounded and left for dead in the First World War, he brought various talents to his links with the Yeomanry, some of them not military – even designing the new guidon for the regiment.

In my twenty years overseeing the estate, I have frequently been reminded of the links between this historic place and its local regiment. It will be my great pleasure later this year to welcome those who have served in the Northamptonshire Yeomanry back, as my guests, to Althorp – 'home' for us all.

The 9th Earl Spencer DL
Patron
The Northamptonshire Yeomanry

CHAPTER ONE

HORSES FOR MY KINGDOM
(1794–1815)

Where are the Yeomen –
the Yeomen of England?
… As foemen may curse them,
No other land could nurse them. (*Merrie England*)

'A horse! A horse! My kingdom for a horse!' cried Richard III, according to Shakespeare. Another more modern playwright featured the 'Mad King', George III, and it was in George's name the cry now went out, not for a single horse but for fifteen thousand: Britain was in mortal peril!

A would-be invader stood at the gates. On Beachy Head and all around the coast the bonfires waited to blaze; bell-ringers had been briefed to send out the warning peal. In Parliament prophecies of doom prevailed as across the Channel an army was massing, landing ships were being built and plans to land on the south coast, in Wales, in Ireland, were being refined. The regular forces on hand to repel invaders were insufficient to the task; a Home Guard was needed.

To make matters worse, an insidious doctrine, like an icy fog propelled by an easterly wind, was seeping in from the Continent. The people over there, a mere 20 miles distant, had dethroned their monarch, sent their aristocracy to the guillotine and established a reign of terror instigated by the ruthless dictator Robespierre, as cruel as Caligula or Nero. The politics proclaimed by the new regime encouraged the downfall of royal houses and the rule of the common people. Such an enticing philosophy might well rouse the poorest in Britain, as food prices rose and unemployment increased; as the rich got richer and the poor got poorer. There was danger of internal strife, riots, a 'break in and help yourself' psychology. The country as a whole had no established police force, no riot squad; a Home Guard was needed! Volunteers – men, horses, swords and carbines.

But this Home Guard was not to be a Dad's Army as the more recent television caricature depicts. No arthritic grandfathers and callow youths; no civilian clothes hastily militarised by donning shabby armbands; no drill with broomsticks or antiquated guns; no makeshift vehicles; no unattractive, sagging battledress once uniforms had tardily arrived; no long delay before this enthusiastic but untrained rabble could be coerced into a well-drilled, if still rather motley force ready to face the enemy when the church bells rang, the beacons flared and the code word circulated. This Home Guard would instantly be flamboyantly uniformed, fully accoutred with lethal weapons, intricately drilled and furnished with towering, plumed helmets to scare the enemy or cow a rioting populace.

The creation of this new force would not be done on the cheap. A receipt for the first forty uniforms for the Northampton Troop reveals the cost of putting a Yeoman into uniform from local funds in 1794. Each uniform was costed as follows:

Coat and waistcoat	£3. 3s.
Leather breeches	£1. 7s.
Boots	£1. 2s.
Hat with bearskin, feather and cockade	£1. 0s.
Total	£6. 12s. (or about £620 in current money)[1]

So, in 1794, Prime Minister William Pitt the Younger called for volunteers, both horsed and foot, fit and of military age, to assemble for service locally. It was to be a well-planned mobilisation, based on the county system and imposing clear and urgent objectives on the highest local authorities. The cavalry contingents would, he said, consist of 'Gentlemen and Yeomanry', and the incentive or coercion for men of high local standing would not be financial gain; indeed, they would be required to contribute lavishly. The compulsion would be the lesson offered by the high authorities across the Channel. They had failed in their trust and now had suffered political oblivion, cruel personal imprisonment and, for many, death.

'Gentlemen' was an easily comprehended term, but who were the 'Yeomanry'? What indeed was a Yeoman? The idea of horsed volunteers was not new, as there had been earlier voluntary units, such as, in Northamptonshire, The King's Carbiniers, or the Duke of Montagu's Horse, raised in Kettering in an earlier war but later disbanded.

What distinguished a Yeoman from any other kind of individual of military age? A simple definition was 'a person who could bring a horse to battle and ride the horse'.

Northamptonshire Yeomanry officer, 1794, in green tunic with buff facings. (*NYA*)

Thus was adapted a term with a long history. Legally, in the 1700s it was 'a person qualified by possessing free land of forty shillings annual rental value [£160 today] to serve on juries, and vote for knights of the shire'. Way back before 1400 the Yeoman was only 'a common menial attendant'. In Chaucer's Middle English period a '*Yoman*' could simply be a young man. To search back through the ages to Old Frisian, pre-Anglo-Saxon, the origin of the word may have been '*Gauman*', with *Gau* meaning a village. By 1794 he would be 'any small farmer or countryman above the grade of labourer'. In terms of the Yeomanry regiments now to be established, townspeople of trader or craftsman standard could also be enrolled if they brought a horse and could stay on its back. Thus a shopkeeper from Kettering could ride boot to boot with a smallholder from Luddington-in-the-Brook. A Northampton brewer could drill with a blacksmith from Brafield-on-the-Green. A Daventry schoolmaster could break bread with a miller from Bugbrooke.

Given twenty-first-century complaints about the inefficiency of the mail or the problems of travel or the dead hand of bureaucracy, the 1794 mobilisation was an amazing example of urgency, commitment and objectivity. On 14 March 1794, Secretary of State Lord Westmorland wrote to all lord lieutenants outlining a plan to raise voluntary cavalry. On 7 April the Militia Bill was given its third reading in Parliament, covering both infantry and cavalry, and all lord lieutenants were instructed to put the plan into action forthwith. By 10 April things began to take shape.

In Northamptonshire the Lord Lieutenant, the 8th Earl of Northampton, was absent at that moment but three deputy lieutenants (DL) requested that the High Sheriff, Richard Booth, call a meeting. This took place in the County Hall on 10 April to discuss a local plan already circulated by Sir William Dolben, DL, a well-known man of action on the national scene. In 1788 he had been the author and prime mover of the act to regulate conditions on board slave ships, which would be enforced by the Royal Navy and was an early step in the abolition of slavery.[2]

The draft plan was read and contained proposals to raise Yeomanry troops of from fifty to eighty men per troop 'for the Purpose of the local Defence of the particular Places where they may be raised'; a person raising two troops was to become a major, four troops a lieutenant colonel and six troops a colonel; the 'Horses to be furnished by the Gentry or Yeomanry who compose the Corps'; to recruit pioneers to assist the horsemen; that the troops also be available 'for the Suppression of Riots and Tumult'; 'that a Subscription be opened to defray the Expense of carrying into Effect such Measures'; that a committee 'may be established in Consequence of these Resolutions'; and that the said committee do meet immediately in the Record Room. The resolutions were moved by Earl Spencer, seconded by Mr W.R. Cartwright and passed unanimously.

Indeed, on 10 April the new committee sat with Earl Spencer in the chair and appointed treasurers and a secretary. It also worked out a rota by which sub-committees should be formed, and recruiting begun of troops in nine towns, including Peterborough which was then in the Northamptonshire electoral district, all to be concluded by the 29th instant. A list of thirty-nine subscribers was formed who offered sums from 5 guineas upward. The list was headed by Earl Spencer who committed £500 (now about £47,000) and the total of that initial 'collection' was £3,217 5s (about £300,000 today). The committee minutes ended with the note that the recruits 'be substantial

Householders who shall engage to bring a Horse to be approved by the Commanding officer of the Troop'. The various troops would become the Northamptonshire 'Corps of Gentleman and Yeomanry', and later the Yeomanry Regiment.

If Sir William Dolben could be described as a man of action on the national scene, then it would apply even more so to George John, 2nd Earl Spencer. He was the outstanding First Lord of the Admiralty who had successfully dealt with historic naval mutinies which had erupted due to bad working conditions. Over the heads of more senior admirals he promoted the relatively young Horatio Nelson to command of the Mediterranean Fleet and therefore contributed greatly to Trafalgar and final victory in the long Napoleonic Wars, while overseeing earlier naval victories. George John had many and varied interests, including the creation one of the largest libraries in the world with 40,000 books at Althorp House. He also founded the Roxburghe Club, still the pre-eminent international association of bibliophiles.

The 2nd Earl Spencer was also a fox-hunting man. There had been a pack of hounds at Althorp for a century and a half, which he continued, and with other enthusiasts he helped to develop the Pytchley Club, later the Pytchley Hunt, which rode over neighbouring areas including the Althorp estate. Fox hunts were responsible for the improvement and training of members' horses to the extent that they would become a prime source for providing suitable horses, both in the Napoleonic Wars and through-

out the First World War. The Northamptonshire Yeomanry over the years would include both masters and hunt staff with their admirable mounts.

The importance of the horses to Yeomanry regiments and the concern which officers felt for their steeds are well illustrated in only the third meeting of the Northamptonshire Yeomanry (NY) Committee, which was held at Earl Spencer's London house on 2 June 1794. Concern was expressed for their fine hunters as it was thought that the regulation military saddle 'may hurt the horse's back'. The committee therefore approved the sum of £1 5s each for the

George John, 2nd Earl Spencer founded the Northamptonshire Yeomanry in 1794. *(Courtesy of Charles, 9th Earl Spencer)*

men to obtain their own more flexible saddles. The attachments, such as girths, stirrups and holsters, would be provided by the regiment.

Meanwhile, by 9 May 1794 the War Office had confirmed officers' commissions. Colonel Spencer was personally raising the Northampton Troop, his lieutenant colonel, Earl Fitzwilliam, recruiting at Peterborough, Major W.R. Cartwright forming Brackley, and sundry captains at Daventry, Kettering, Oundle and Towcester. As early as 17 May more than 200 volunteers on horseback attended an initial rally commanded by Earl Spencer, before drinks at the Peacock Inn, setting up a pleasurable precedent. Within a few days Earl Fitzwilliam carried out a first inspection of the Peterborough Troop, consisting of sixty men on horseback, after which refreshment was sought at the Angel Inn. That evening a ball was given by the Gentlemen of the Troop for the ladies of the city and this was 'very genteely attended'.

One great attraction in recruitment was the colourful, even gaudy design of the uniform of a troop or a regiment, and poets were already at work writing patriotic songs. On 4 June a Brackley troop had been enrolled and met for their first 'military evolutions', surely one of the earliest exercises by Yeomanry. Afterwards they retired to the Crown Inn where, after loyal toasts, they sang in 'the most convivial and harmonious manner' about their uniform, although whether it was already available to wear, and whether they would ever wield broadswords, is rather doubtful. No doubt over their beers they bellowed:

> British Yeomen, valiant Yeomen, brave Yeomen for ever
> Green coats faced with black and in each hat a feather
> Their waistcoats are buff and their trousers are leather
> With broadswords and pistols and hearts without fear
> Great Jove must be pleased when these Yeomen appear.

The 1794 roll of the Northampton Troop, under Earl Spencer as colonel, shows a captain, a cornet (junior lieutenant), a quartermaster (QM) and two sergeants plus eighty Yeomen, while the Brackley troop under Major W.R. Cartwright, had a lieutenant, a cornet and forty-two Yeomen. There were a number of fathers and sons or brothers enlisted together, such as John and Samuel Pell of Overstone and John H. Pell, of Sywell; S.H. and John Butterfield at Brackley; William and John Lathbury; Henry and John Webb; and various Waltons, Marriotts and Butlins. Two worthies by the name of Aris, a surname well known in the 1940s through Jack Aris, 1NY, a corporal cook and great character at more recent Association reunions.

The colour and design of tunics and hats was left to the individual commanders as units sprang up all over Britain. On 31 May Earl Spencer received a letter from Lord Carnarvon asking for advice, as his Lordship was forming the Yeomanry in Wiltshire. The Wiltshires, who would become the senior Yeomanry regiment by dint of continuous service, came into being on 4 June 1794 at a meeting in the Bear Inn, Devizes, at the call of Richard Long, High Sheriff of Wiltshire. Troops sprang up around the coast, particularly at towns in Kent, although the entire coastal population felt menaced. Had not the Spanish Armada sailed right around the British Isles? In Pembrokeshire, the Lord Lieutenant, Lord Milford, recruited the nucleus of a regiment; in Ayrshire the Earl of

Brackley troop officer and trooper in green tunic with buff facings, 1790s. *(NYA)*

Cassillis formed a troop; inland, other counties also responded, with Captain John Somers-Cocks forming the Worcestershire's first troop at the Unicorn Inn in Worcester, favouring a spectacular Hussars tunic of bright red with white facings. An elaborate Hussar design was also selected in Oxfordshire. It was rather later, and possibly with an eye more on civil disobedience than foreign invasion, that the first London troop appeared in Uxbridge.[3]

Whilst national and county authorities drove relentlessly on towards a War Office total of 15,120 Yeomanry cavalry in 1798, junior officers and non-commissioned officers (NCOs) wrestled with the growing problems of a new organisation. The troops in Northamptonshire needed an expert military horseman to lick them into shape in the way that infantry regimental sergeant majors (RSMs) drilled foot soldiers to perfection. After advertisements and enquiries, Thomas Pickering was discovered. He had already served for more than twenty years with the Household Cavalry, latterly as their riding master, and would now contribute another twenty years' service to the Yeomanry in Northamptonshire. He, like all other Yeomen, would go on to a fixed remuneration scale, starting at 2s 9d per day of duty rendered. (In 1942 the author joined up on 3s a day, but the 1794 allowance was worth far more for part-time attendance!) Yeomen would also gain other perks, including exemption from paying toll charges if in uniform and also from a tax on the white wig powder so often used by dandies of the time.

Captain Arnold in Daventry lacked a suitable troop sergeant, so he placed an advert in the *Mercury* newspaper on 14 June 1794 calling for a qualified person. A response came from former regular sergeant Samuel Clitsey, who was considered suitable despite lacking a thumb. Now very happy, the Daventry Troop paraded next time with their worthy, single-thumbed troop sergeant. Clitsey's horse, an unfamiliar steed of an anarchic disposition, promptly reared up and threw the sergeant heavily. His leg was broken so badly that he had to resign from the troop forthwith. Captain Arnold placed another advert in the *Mercury*.

There seems to have been no great problem with the provision of arms for the first troops raised. A trooper's armament consisted of a carbine, about the size of a modern rifle, together with a bayonet and rammer to muzzle-load the gun; a rather complicated large pistol with a bore the size of a carbine's; and a sword, initially some of them straight but usually of the slightly curved sabre type. Then there was the question of the distinguishing badge. In some cases, county units simply took the county badge as their emblem. With a voice at court, Earl Spencer petitioned the king for use of the king's own badge, the galloping 'White Horse of Hanover'. This was graciously approved, the NY being one of four military formations to be allowed to wear that emblem.

The next priority was the standard around which the unit would rally. For the cavalry the appropriate form of flag was, and still is, the guidon – an oblong shape with a triangular segment cut out of the leading edge. This is seen very much as a royal honour gracing the regiment, squadron or troop. Amid all his other activities, Earl Spencer gave his attention to the design and production of the regiment's first three guidons. On 5 October 1795 Messrs Cox and Greenwood presented their invoice for 'three standards and paint, with proper badges, arms and etc. Gold fringe and tassels, staves and cases and 3 cornet belts, gold laced. Total £41.0.0.'

Thus it was possible on Saturday 17 October 1795 for the local *Mercury* to report:

> This town has been witness to many a public scene that pleased the eye and interested the heart; but safely may we assert that never were the inhabitants more pleased, or their hearts more gratified, than by the splendid scene which took place on the general review of the regiment of Yeomanry, by their Colonel, and the delivery of the Standards by Lady Spencer. All appeared Love, Loyalty and Unanimity. So deeply did the spectators enter into the spirit of the show that it was only after it was all over they recollected the morning was wet and unfavourable for a public spectacle.

The regiment had assembled on the racecourse before riding into town. There, three cornets 'had the distinguished honour of having the standard belt put over their shoulders by the fair hands of their patriotic countrywomen'. Lady Spencer then handed the standards 'with inimitable grace' to the colonel who delivered each to the proper officer. With an eye to current politics, the chaplain, Reverend Bailey, prayed that the Yeomen would 'stand forth in support' of, among other priorities, the 'Constitution

Presentation of three guidons by 'the ladies', 1795. *(Tout)*

under which, through thine infinite goodness, these kingdoms have hitherto prospered, and which, by thy gracious Providence, they may be enabled to maintain, and to transmit, unimpaired, to their latest posterity'.

At the presentation of the first guidon to the Gloucestershire Gentlemen and Yeomanry the chaplain, the vicar of Cheltenham, was much more poetic than Reverend Bailey, although still assuming that God would provide similar reinforcement, declaiming:

> Lurks here sedition in her murky cell,
> With whom congenial imps of darkness dwell.
> Your magic swords shall, like Ithuriel's spear,
> Detect the monster in her foul career.
> 'Tis yours kind friends, to guard with tender care,
> And shield from brutal insolence the Fair;
> The brightest actions from these sources spring
> Truth, friendship, Love, our altars and our King.[4]

In Northampton Earl Spencer addressed the troops with obvious pride, acknowledging 'the unwearied pains, which, it was evident to the delighted eye of every spectator, they had taken since he last saw them, which gave him the most sensible satisfaction'. He then took his place at the head of the column, with the 'several standards flying at the head of each squadron' as they returned to the 'race-ground'. For the ladies there was 'a very elegant cold collation' prepared in the grandstand, but the troops themselves were released to the George Inn and the Peacock Inn, where their consumption of roast beef and beers led to more loyal toasts and exuberant singing, including:

> Success to our Fleets and our Armies who roam
> Likewise our brave Yeomen who guard us at home
> May George long be King and his Subjects be free
> And Fame sound the praise of his brave Yeomanry.

Another of their songs included the significant lines: 'And Northamptonshire Yeomen … have like Britons come forward, to humble all those, who are Englishmen bred, yet are Englishmen's foes.' Even before the presentation of the guidons the NY had been called out on civil disturbance duty. In April 1793 the price of wheat in Northampton had been 42s a bushel, but by August 1795 it had risen to 108s a bushel. The price of bread rose accordingly, as did the cost of other essentials, and this led to inevitable protests. Then on 4 April 1795, near Queen Eleanor's Cross, Northampton, as food wagons approached the town:

A numerous body of people proceeded to cut open the butter flats [wagons], the contents of which, as well as a quantity of meat, they carried off. In a short time all the Yeomanry who reside in the town, attended by their officers, J.H. Thursby, jnr, and R.B. Cox esqr., were on horseback, completely acoutred and ready to give assistance to return order … but the crowd soon dispersed.

So there was already a call for local action in civil situations. And it is highly likely that the rampaging civilians at Queen Eleanor's Cross were less impelled by French republican philosophy than by sheer common hunger. But if the average Yeoman was dreaming of glorious cavalry charges at the gallop against the republican Frenchmen, they were, in the vast majority, likely to be disappointed. Under Carnot, who followed Robespierre and preceded Napoleon as French head of state, there were certainly serious plans afoot in 1796 for an invasion of the British Isles.

In fact the young rising military star, Napoleon Bonaparte, had refused the opportunity of invading England and the task reverted to Colonel William Tate, an elderly Irish-American. The French War Minister, General Hoche, raised a *Seconde Legion de France*, mainly from specially pardoned prisoners and deserters, which led to the formation being termed the 'Black Legion'. Ships were provided to convey these troops, not to the nearest Kent or Sussex coast, but to Wales and Ireland. The latter attack was aimed at creating an independent pro-French Ireland and, at the same time, a Welsh landing would gain a bridgehead on the mainland: Britain would be attacked through the back door from a firm Irish base. The western section of the French fleet had aimed to land in the Bristol Channel, but adverse winds drove it north to Cardigan Bay. Sailing under British colours, those ships anchored at Carreg Wasted Point, near Fishguard, on Wednesday 22 February 1797, hoisted the French tricolour and disembarked. Tate set up defence points on Carn Wynda and Carn Gelli hills but, as the French soldiers had not been provided with food supplies, they immediately began to disperse and forage widely. Some soldiers located a farmhouse stocked with wine from a smuggler's boat which had been wrecked on Pencaer Rocks. The lucky lads began to imbibe.[5]

At 11 p.m. that night Lord Cawdor was alerted at his home nearby. There were volunteer infantry available under the young Lieutenant Colonel Thomas Knox, but he had no military experience, so Cawdor appointed the more experienced Lord Milford, captain of the Castlemartin Yeomanry Cavalry, to command the defence. Meanwhile, the French troops had been dismayed to see their ships sail away and leave them at the mercy of whatever armies might assemble against them. The French admiral Castagnier intended to cross to Ireland to land more troops there. At this point the British Navy intervened and the French infantry around Fishguard were effectively marooned. Had they been experienced, disciplined troops they would still have been a formidable, well-armed invasion force.

Against the invaders Lord Milford had a motley but spectacular little army. Many civilians had rallied to the scene carrying makeshift weapons such as farm implements. The militia infantry formed up in drilled lines. On horseback the Castlemartin Yeomanry in their splendid uniforms were an impressive sight. It is not known precisely if it was an idea of Lord Milford's but, spontaneous or planned, a force of 400 Welsh women in red flannel cloaks and traditional tall hats marched into sight. One of the women, Jemima Nicholas, a tall 47-year-old cobbler armed with a pitchfork, had already rounded up and captured a dozen of the foraging enemy.

On the French side, Tate and the planners had hoped that their invasion would provoke revolutionary anarchy among the depressed and desperate local population. Now, as one report describes it, 'the French troops had not shown any real inclination to fight but a strong inclination to drink. Lord Cawdor called for an unconditional

Castlemartin Yeomanry (on horseback) receive surrender of French in ranks (centre) – battle honour 'Fishguard'. *(Pembrokeshire Museum / Dyfed)*

surrender and the invaders laid down their arms. The success of the defenders' bluff, and the danger which might have developed, is illustrated by the fact that the local people collected about fifty-five cartloads of French weapons from Goodwick Sands after the surrender. The Castlemartin (Pembrokeshire) Yeomanry thus became the only Yeomanry to be in action against the French and have since proudly carried the unique battle honour 'Fishguard' on their guidons.

For other Yeomanry regiments it was a less glorious routine of drills and occasional call-outs, either in a moment of abortive national emergency or some minor civil disturbance. One such incident caused the call-out of the Northampton and Althorp troops in July 1799, the official account stated that 'in consequence of some obstructions which the Commissioners, [responsible] for dividing and enclosing the open field of Wilbarton, have met with from a number of persons claiming right of common in the said fields – who not only avowed their determination to resist the fencing-out of a piece of land allotted to them in lieu of the common right, but had even set the civil power at defiance'. The Yeomanry troops were commanded by Major Cartwright, accompanied by Reverend Mr Griffin, magistrate, and 'having under escort a wagon loaded with posts and rails for fencing out the above allotment'. The Yeomen found a 'mob of about 300 persons', who had lit a large bonfire in the road to obstruct the wagons. The magistrate then read the Riot Act and, after waiting an hour to allow tempers, and fire, to cool somewhat, the troops were ordered to advance with the wagon. One or two of 'the most active of the mob were taken into custody and compelled to assist in setting down the posts and rails'. The Yeomanry then stood by for about three hours, during which the greatest part of the crowd had dispersed and 'the workmen were left in quiet possession of the field'. There were no reports of casualties or further penalties against protesters and the Yeomen rankers were paid their 2s 9d each.

In 1798, T. Dicey & Co. printers and publishers had found it worthwhile to produce a twenty-six-page booklet entitled 'PLAN OF EXERCISE for the Northamptonshire Yeomen Cavalry'. This reveals the complicated drill moves which the huntsmen and smallholders of the county were expected to learn and perfect. It includes formations, sword exercises, wheeling manoeuvres and even the format for a march past at a general's inspection. The spontaneous and rumbustious enthusiasm of the hunt would be replaced by the regulated and schematic discipline of the parade ground.

One complicated evolution awaiting the rough riders was preceded by the cautionary order 'Form Squadron on the right division by the oblique march …' Then a succession of orders: 'Divisions on the right back half wheel – March! … Halt! … Dress!' These loudly shouted commands should produce the following wheel:

> The right division stands fast – the other divisions will be ordered to wheel back on the reverse flank, as much as is necessary to place that flank perpendicularly to its point in line – the conducting Officers having placed themselves on that flank, the whole will march; and as each division arrives within twenty or twenty-five paces of the line, its conducting Officer gives the word 'Left shoulder, forward!' to which the man next to himself gradually turns his horse, so as to arrive in the line perpendicularly square to his own person, and the rest of his division conforming to him, and proportionately quickening their pace arrive in full parallel front on the line. The Officer then gives the word 'Halt! Dress up!' and changes to his post in squadron.

At which point, during the first trial parade, it might be assumed that the smallholder from Luddington-in-the Brook, the blacksmith from Brafield-on-the-Green, the miller from Bugbrooke and even the schoolmaster from Daventry, together with their horses, more inured to choosing each its own gap in the hedge ahead in pursuit of the baying hounds, would all feel a little disorientated in seeking the perpendicular. Perhaps riding master Pickering wished he had remained with the Household Cavalry and Troop Sergeant Clitsey glad that he had broken his leg so badly. It is not surprising that a note suggests that 'attention must be paid to placing intelligent men on the flanks of divisions'.

Consideration was given to the demands upon the rankers of their civilian occupations, especially at harvest time, and individual troops varied their programmes as necessary. Where possible longer periods of combined training were arranged, but not yet the annual camps of later days. On 18 September 1801 the Northampton troop, having lost parade time due to harvesting, was summoned to train full time for three days, Monday to Wednesday. At this time rumours were circulating of a possible peace treaty with the French. On Saturday 21 November 1801, Earl Spencer paraded his troops and advised them that 'though there was every prospect of the peace being soon finally concluded, yet that till the Definitive Treaty was signed they should hold themselves in constant readiness'. He also thanked them for their 'respectable appearance and cheerful attendance'.

It seems that even at that time newspapers were not averse to quoting from 'sources'. Recording that the parade had ended with 'three loud huzzas', the reporter went on to say: 'We understand from a hint dropped by his Lordship that he was not prepared then to say what would be His Majesty's further pleasure concerning them when the Definitive Treaty was signed.' It was on another Saturday, 24 July 1802, that the earl informed the Yeomen of the provisions of the signed Treaty of Amiens and the possibility of continuing service even during peacetime. The reporter's version revealed that there was a certain amount of democratic choice in the destiny of Yeomanry regiments at that time:

> If the Regiment should in general conceive that the object for which they been originally formed was already attained, and that no important purpose would be answered by their further continuance, he should readily acquiesce in their determination, but on the other hand, of they should, with him, think that so respectable and constitutional a corps as the Yeomanry would, even in times of Peace, prove of essential service, both to procuring the continuance of the Peace and increasing the internal security of the Country, he should with great pleasure resume his command of a body of men who were entitled to his warmest appreciation and sincere acknowledgements of their constant attention to him.

His Lordship's words were received with 'loud acclamations', which no doubt redoubled when he announced that 'two fat bucks' were already turning on the spits at the Peacock Inn 'awaiting their acceptance'. Before dealing with the two fat bucks, enough men signalled their intention to continue service that the local troops were immediately filled up to establishment level. So it was with great gusto that loyal toasts were drunk, including 'May we never be weary of well-doing'. This led on to more of the songs which were now familiar to all ranks:

> The Northamptonshire Yeoman, with high mettl'd steeds
> Should occasion present, would display noble deeds
> And boldly chastise every foe to the cause
> Of our King, our Religion, our Freedom and Laws.

> Both Yeomen and horse are equally good
> And if e'er they're opposed they will prove British blood:
> With broadswords and pistol they'll make their foes fly
> For the true British Yeomen will conquer or die.

For those who desired peace and a quiet existence, the ambitions of Napoleon produced an unwelcome shock as war broke out again on 18 May 1803. Napoleon had now become the First Consul of France. He had also annexed Piedmont and Elba, and was refusing to withdraw French troops from the Netherlands. This was seen as a direct threat to Britain and caused a renewal of hostilities. The Northants volunteers again subscribed to the 'Articles of Enrolment' originally published on 3 May 1794. One interesting article allowed that 'personnel desirous of furnishing a Substitute … may do so on condition that he be a Man of good Character, having a fixed residence in the County; that he be accustomed to Riding … and that he be approved of by a Majority of those Persons who compose the Troop in which he is to serve', again revealing the rather democratic nature of service. The Notes and Explanations of the formal contract enlarge on the ponderous legal terms:

(a) Substantial Householders, or their sons, whether Farmers, Tradesmen, or of any other Occupation, may enrol their names.

(b) ... the Days of Exercise shall not be oftener than once a Week, unless with the general consent of the Persons called ... Weekly exercise will be dispensed with during Hay-Time and Harvest.

(c) The Corps ... can be marched out of the County into any Part of the Kingdom only in Case of actual Invasion, and into any adjoining County only in Aid of any similar Corps for the Suppression of Riots and Tumults ...

(d) Those who shall enrol ... are not obliged to incur any other Expence than the Maintenance of themselves and their Horse.

(e) The Approbation of a Majority of those serving in Person in any Troop being required for any Substitute, the Yeomen are effectually secured against the Admission of any Person with whom they may not wish to associate.

(f) As the Officers ... [who are] entitled to Pay, engage to put it into one general Stock-Purse for all ... the daily Allowance of every person ... will be augmented considerably beyond the Pay allowed by Government to the regular Light Cavalry.

Yeomen of the First World War and especially those conscripted in the latter years of the Second World War would no doubt have been both surprised and delighted if they had been able to refuse to serve with someone whom they disliked, and if they knew that officers' pay was going into a common 'Stock-Purse' to enhance their own meagre remittance.

On 2 December 1804 Napoleon assumed the title of Emperor of the French, and by 1805 he had 132,000 soldiers and 2,000 sea-going craft assembled at Boulogne for an invasion of Britain; the Yeomanry might still be needed on the beaches of Britain. Measures were taken to ensure that the county Yeomanry regiments maintained a high level of military readiness. In September 1805 the Northampton men were inspected by Lieutenant General Gwynn, as the first of a series of inspections by regular officers from the rank of colonel upwards on a quarterly basis. At the moment of a national call-out, all Northants troops were to rendezvous centrally as one body at the Market Hall in Northampton.

Training of Yeomanry in the use of firearms in battle was in some ways more complicated than training with modern small arms. To state the obvious, shooting a pistol from horseback is more difficult than shooting a pistol from a tank turret: the tank does not shy away when a pistol is fired between its ears, nor does the tank suddenly decide to veer in the opposite direction from the one to which the driver is aiming. But even dismounted, the firearms of the 1800s were awkward and time-consuming to fire.

The carbine, which might hit a target at between 50 and 100 yards, required several actions to fire successive shots. The troops' carbines were best fired as a united volley rather than single shots by individuals, which required further training over and above the burden of actually firing the gun. The process of loading and firing went as follows:

'*Load!*' Make a quarter face to the right, drawing the right foot back six inches, bring the left hand smartly across the body, grasp the carbine a little above the gripe [buckle of the sling], and bring it down with the butt against the outside of the left leg and resting on the swivel, the barrel turned towards the front, the muzzle pointed forward and opposite to the middle of the chest, the right hand holding and steadying the muzzle.

'*Handle Cartridge!*' Carry the hand to the pouch, take hold of a cartridge, draw it out and bite off the end.

'*Two!*' Bring the right hand down to the muzzle; shake the powder into the barrel, put in the paper and the ball; and then take hold of the head of the ramrod with the fore finger and thumb.

'*Draw Ramrod!*' Draw out the ramrod and put it into the barrel about six inches.

'*Ram Down Cartridge!*' Push the cartridge to the bottom.

'*Return Ramrod!*' Draw the ramrod out of the barrel, and restore it into the pipe, forcing it well home; the fore finger and thumb still holding the ramrod.

'*Prime!*' Bring the carbine to the 'priming position' against the right side, the muzzle raised as high as the upper part of the peak of the cap or helmet, but pointing directly to the front; the left hand across the body holding the carbine at the gripe, and the thumb a little above the swivel-bar; the thumb of the right hand placed upon the cock, the fingers behind the guard, half-cock the carbine (here removing an old cap, if there be one), and then grasp the small of the butt.

'*Two!*' Carry the right hand to the cap pocket, take out a cap and place it on the nipple, the thumb pressing on the cap with the fingers shut.

'*Ready!*' Place the thumb of the right hand upon the cock, the fingers behind the guard; cock the carbine and grasp the small of the butt.

'*Present!*' Raise the carbine steadily to the 'Present' and look along the barrel; place the fore finger before the trigger but avoid touching it, the carbine well pressed to the shoulders by the three last fingers of the right hand.

'*Fire!*' By the action of the fingers alone, and by a gradual but firm pressure, pull the trigger and remain looking along the piece.

At that point the carbine might fire if, in the meantime, it had not rained and wet the powder. Whilst the entire operation took several seconds, it would give the gunner opportunity for perhaps two shots before a person on foot could approach from about 50 yards away. As the general issue pistol was equipped with a similar cocking and firing mechanism to that of the carbine, much of the carbine firing drill was used also for the pistol. The pistol instructions commenced with a reminder, on the command '*Draw Pistol!*', to take off the right-hand glove, unbutton the flounce, push forward the cloak, or draw back the sheepskin and *shabraque* (saddle cloth) according to the equipment, and passing the right hand under the left arm, seize the butt of the pistol. To fire, the pistol must be 'nearly as high as, and in line with the right eye, with the muzzle lowered to the object; the hand lightly grasping the butt, the arm a little bent, and without stiffness'.

Once the mechanical movements for firing the carbine and pistol had been mastered on foot, there came the problem of carrying out the same movements on the back of a very sensitive living creature, often of revolutionary tendencies. The text-book admonition proposed the following safeguards:

Yeomanry with muzzle-loading carbines and sabres up to 1870. *(Worcestershire Yeomany Enacters)*

In all the motions connected with firing, great care must be taken to avoid altering the accustomed feeling of the bridle in the horse's mouth, or the usual seat and balance of the man. And the position of his legs, as tending to alarm the animal; for a horse once rendered timid by an accident in firing from his back will make the practice of it both difficult and dangerous. When the recruit is familiar with the firings at the halt he is then to practise them while his horse is in motion. Great care must be taken that, in presenting to the front or left, he does not strike or touch the horses' head with the Carbine or Pistol.[6]

Similarly for the Yeoman recruit, swordsmanship was not a simple matter of 'bash and slash'. As he learned the routine, on foot at first, he could not move about or take evasive action as in the athletic pursuit of fencing. He must turn, bend or stoop, from the hips only, without twisting the legs and feet, as would be necessary when fixed in the saddle. Thus immobilised he would use a system of cuts and guards. There was general advice, such as for the 'Cut' where the effective part of the blade is about 6in from the point; for the 'Guard', oppose to the adversary the half nearest the hilt; hold the sword flexible in the hand (not an instinctive reaction) as no strength is gained by too stiff a grasp. Then on to drill by numbers.

The drill commenced with positions of the sword: draw, slope, carry, prove distance (from adversary), engage, recover, port, salute and return (to scabbard). There were seven different 'Cuts' (or slashes) and three different 'Points' (or stabs). On the receiving end, there were seven 'Guards', a 'Parry' and a 'Left Defend'. Once these basic moves had been mastered they then had to be practised both on foot and on horseback. A further step to battle readiness consisted of practising as a division, with all men responding in unison to a standard series of command shouts from an officer. The combination of 'Guards', 'Cuts' and 'Points' in each series could change at the whim of the commander. There is, remarkably, no record of horses' ears being lopped off at early stages of recruits' mounted practice.

Napoleon was still kicking his heels at Boulogne while waiting for his navy to gain control of the seas. But in 1805 the church bells of Britain rang with the news of a magnificent victory which would secure control of the seas for Britain and her ally, Portugal: the Battle of Trafalgar. Almost immediately, the bells had to be muffled to toll the calamitous news that the nation's great sailor hero, Admiral Lord Nelson, had been killed at the moment of victory. An extraordinary tide of mourning swept the country in a manner seen only rarely in the nation's history. From the War Office an invitation, with the weight of an instruction, went out to Yeomanry regiments to provide details which would stand in full ceremonial dress along the route of the approaching funeral. The Yeomen from various counties would form as a regiment and be stationed on the west side of Temple Bar en route from the Admiralty to St Paul's Cathedral.

The funeral took place of 9 January 1806, and the Yeomanry stood at the point where the Lord Mayor received the procession. The regular bands caused 'muffled drums to roll' and 'music to play solemn dirges occasionally'. The Yeomen, in their varying hues of splendid dress, wore black crape 'on the left arm below the elbow' as they stood two deep, charged with 'ensuring that no unauthorised individuals joined the procession' and not to 'suffer any carriage to enter the Grand Route except those forming the procession'. In this sad and solemn setting the still infant Yeomanry was afforded its only great opportunity for ostentation and public display, even though dismounted, on a national scene during the wars which lasted until 1815.[7]

The hostilities between 1789 and 1815 had been something of a 'stop and go' sequence. There had been the 'Peace' of Amiens in 1802; in April 1814, with France on the verge of defeat, Napoleon had been removed from the French throne and sent in the guise of a governor, but virtually exiled, to the small island of Elba – the war appeared to be at an end. After the celebrated 'Hundred Days' Napoleon returned to France, regained power and mobilised an army to start another war. On 18 June 1815 he was defeated at Waterloo and sent into exile on St Helena in the remote south Atlantic. But he was still alive, relatively young and still popular in his native France. Was this really the end of the Napoleonic Wars?

This uncertainty led to many Yeomanry regiments continuing to function for another decade, rather than being demobilised immediately after the 1815 treaty. In addition to a possible foreign threat, there was also an internal dilemma. Although France had reverted from its aggressive and proselytising republicanism of the 1790s to a traditional Bourbon monarchy, there was still mounting pressure for political reform within Britain itself. This was accompanied by the threat of civil strife due to unemployment, food shortages and tardy reform measures. In this respect, the Yeomanry might still be needed in its 'Riot Squad' role during times of peace.

CHAPTER TWO

CALL OUT THE RIOT SQUAD!
(1815–1899)

For the new Yeomanry regiments peacetime meant a gentle routine of regular training parades interrupted occasionally by the more dramatic episodes of call-out. The call-outs were divided between 'Riots' and 'Royals', mounted police duties or escorts to visiting dignitaries. The regular army was mainly occupied by colonial wars, with one major conflict, the Crimean War, occurring midway through the century. Some Yeomanry regiments lapsed into what was officially termed 'suspended animation', but which one historian has called 'glamorous inactivity'. There may have been some glamour in the splendid uniforms but there was no opportunity for military glory.

However, in 1819 one Northamptonshire 'Gentleman Yeoman', James, Lord Brudenelle volunteered to raise a Deene troop and thus qualified for the rank of captain. On 14 December forty-six of his men were measured for jackets and overalls to his own design, he being a man of taste in matters of couture, and on 10 February 1920 arms were issued to the troop. For the adventurous James, Yeomanry parades were not considered thrilling enough and, after inheriting the title of the Earl of Cardigan, he purchased a colonelcy. In the Crimea he was to lead the infamous 'Charge of the Light Brigade', which galloped at the enemy guns on mistaken orders and at great cost, with 'cannon to the left of them, cannon to the right of them'. Although the horsemen overran the guns the attack failed because of a lack of infantry. (The 2NY and other yeomanry regiments were to suffer equivalent losses in July 1944 due to similar lack of sufficient infantry with enemy guns on all sides. Do generals not read history?) Perhaps the earl's more laudable claim to fame relates to his invention of the article of clothing named after him, the humble cardigan.

In Britain it was a time of increasing civilian discontent. New types of machinery caused unemployment; only about 2 per cent of people enjoyed the right to vote in parliamentary elections; there were food shortages and rising food prices were blamed on the Corn Laws. Some reaction to such conditions was spontaneous and localised, while other uprisings were better organised and spread more widely. In rural areas there was much anger because newly developed threshing machines replaced the traditional labour-intensive manual work which provided winter income for many families. A mysterious Captain Swing wrote threatening letters to landowners and the following period of violence became known as the Swing Riots.

Twenty-nine different Yeomanry uniforms reflecting individual colonels' choices. *(NYA)*

In its role as an extempore 'Riot Squad', there being no appropriate police force, the Yeomanry gained a bad press which has persisted to this day. The ugly side of riot policing led to the so-called Battle of Peterloo. This took place at St Peter's Field in Manchester on 16 August 1819 when the Manchester Patriotic Union organised a huge rally at which a notable radical orator, Henry Hunt, was to speak. Some reports speak of people gathering quietly in their Sunday best. Others reported activists marching in columns to music, carrying flags and slogans. Eventually a crowd, estimated variously at 50,000 to 80,000, assembled around the cart from which Hunt was to give his oration. The extraordinary size of the crowd caused the magistrates to panic before any undue violence had occurred. They ordered the arrest of the leaders, but the special constables refused to act. The nearest troops were the Manchester and Salford Yeomanry and their captain, Hugh Birley, was ordered to make the arrests. Birley was a businessman of Draconian disposition and not likely to shirk such a duty.

The event has generally been reported as all innocence on one side and all vicious violence on the other. Recent events tend to suggest that, where there is a focus of great anger, however justified, other malign elements find an opportunity to disturb what might have been intended as a peaceful demonstration. When the magistrates saw the Yeomanry engulfed in the vast crowd, which, no doubt, was in a dangerous state of increasing anger, fear and panic, they ordered in the regular cavalry. Later the official inquiry into the incident produced a 'whitewash', but the statistics were horrifying. Somewhere between fifteen and eighteen people were killed and perhaps around 500 injured. Those killed included a 2-year-old child and two special constables.

Although the event failed to produce any immediate improvements, rather an increasingly severe response from the government, its story resonated through the radical movement as being a crucial moment in the fight for reform.[1] One lasting outcome was that radical local businessmen founded the *Manchester Guardian* (now the *Guardian*) to promote their views.

History has been less than kind to the Yeomanry in failing to notice many other occasions when protests developed into gratuitous violence which called for calm and fortitude on the part of the relatively small Yeomanry detachments brought in to quell such outbreaks. In the same year as Peterloo, the Kettering Troop was called out to deal with a bread riot. The magistrates read the Riot Act before the Yeomanry then slowly dispersed the crowd without casualties by acting in the correct style as laid down in Standing Orders, which were not followed by the impetuous Yeomanry at Peterloo:

> When formed in line and called upon to advance against a body of rioters ... steadiness and order will produce much more effect and intimidation than any misplaced impetuosity ... never to permit more than one half of the line to advance for the dispersion of rioters, the other half perfectly steady ... at a walk or very gentle trot ... and do not expose themselves to fall into confusion by attempting too great rapidity of movement ... they are irresistible. No ordinary assemblage will be able to prevent mounted Troops advancing, if they preserve good order and silence.[2]

A situation quite different to the Peterloo assembly confronted the then Yeomen Cavalry of Gloucestershire and Monmouth. This focused on the opening of Bristol Assizes on 29 October 1831 at a time when the House of Lords had rejected the Reform Bill passed by the Commons. A crowd had gathered to protest against the Recorder, Sir Charles Wetherell, who was also an MP. The protests gradually descended into mob rule while the regular cavalry, acting as escort, held back and failed to intervene in time to take control. Many of the principal buildings in the city were destroyed, the prison broken open, prisoners released and the authorities in total retreat. Access to stores of alcohol produced a scene where drunken rioters died in fires started by themselves.

The eventual sporadic action by the regular troops caused fatal casualties among the rioters, whose reaction vacillated between momentary dispersal and random outbreaks of increased violence. Desperate messages were sent to the local Yeomanry officers: at Tetbury, Yeomen were called out of the church service on Captain Estcourt's orders; at Doddington, Captain Codrington, informed of the situation at 3 p.m., had sent messengers out into his rural area 'some miles in different directions' and gathered his force by 7 p.m. The Yeomanry troops then carried out a steady advance as prescribed and were effective in the eventual pacifying of the city. The two officers commanding the regular troops were censured, one being cashiered and the other committing suicide. The Yeomanry were thanked by the mayor for 'the promptitude, alacrity and zeal ... in preserving the lives and property of the Citizens and restoring tranquillity'.[3]

On 27 April 1838 the House of Commons debated the future of the Yeomanry and high feelings were roused, as Viscount Howick moved a vote of £80,280 (£7 million in the present day) to defray expenses of the volunteer corps for the next year. Mr Hume MP produced a letter which supported his view that 'he had always objected to the

The Yeomanry face the rioters – 1790s onward. *(Tout)*

yeomanry, because it was a partisan force and one which was not favourably regarded by the public'. The debate continued:

> Mr *Hume*: Hon Members might say 'no, no!' but they could not deny … this circumstance proved that these were partisan corps [No, no.] He said 'yes, yes!' Let hon. Members cry 'no, no!' till they were tired, the facts would speak for themselves … and he thought it was high time to put down the force.
>
> Mr *Benett* being probably the oldest member of the yeomanry corps in that House … had served forty years in that force. The Wiltshire Yeomanry had performed good service … agricultural riots were very different from those in manufacturing places: the agricultural labourers were most persevering and active … The corps behaved with great perseverance and leniencies towards the parties.
>
> Mr *A. Sanford* agreed. It was well worthy of consideration that in an adjoining district, in which the collieries were situated, the yeomanry had been called out no less then fifty times.
>
> Mr *Bagge* could not listen in silence to the attacks … The whole body of the independent yeomanry would throw back with contempt the aspersions made.[4]

In 1828 the Northamptonshire regiment of Yeomanry had been disbanded, thus losing its precedence in the military lists, although by 1831 eight independent local troops had been raised. Contributions to the county Yeomanry fund had been so generous that there was now a question as to the dispersal of superfluous cash. St Andrew's Hospital, Northampton, has on record that 'the Governors of Northampton Infirmary were

informed at a public meeting at the George Inn by Sir William Wake that the subscribers to the Northamptonshire Yeomanry had decided that the surplus fund of £6,000
[£550,000 today] should be given to the Asylum fund'. Actually £7,000 was donated
to buy the land on which the General Lunatic Asylum was built, now St Andrew's. A
note in the deeds implies that if ever St Andrew's is closed the land should revert from
the NHS to the NY.

On the international front, Napoleon III had assumed the throne of France, rousing
fears of renewed French ambitions and leading to national call-outs of the Yeomanry
in 1848, 1851 and 1859. It was deemed necessary that the regiments and independent
troops should be trained and maintained to requirements sometimes different to those
appropriate for action against civilian rioters. The relaxed self-discipline of the earliest
Yeomanry units might not always be sufficient and firm regulations were imposed.

There was a graded system of fines ranging from 10s (2012 = £45) for a commissioned officer to 2s (£9) for a private for offences such as absence from parade, lateness
on parade (one-quarter of the standard fine for every quarter of an hour late), talking in
the ranks, or appearing with horse appointments dirty. Failure to pay fines could cause
a Justice of the Peace to impose a levy of double the amount in cash or by sale of the
defaulter's goods.

One commander told his troops that 'whenever he heard of a man absenting himself
in future, he should issue a warrant for this arrest and send a policeman to execute it'.
There was also a final last resort, the public naming and shaming of a defaulter. A troop
commander was able to use the local newspaper, in this case the *Gloucester Journal*, to
publish a naming and shaming notice:

> SIR – You are requested to insert this Notice:
> 'Thomas Jordan of Cheltenham was dismissed this morning from the Cheltenham
> Troop of Yeomanry Cavalry, now stationed here on permanent duty, for disorderly,
> unsoldierlike conduct, and disobedience of orders.'
>
> I am. Sir, your obedient servant,
> THOMAS GRAY, *Captain*.
> Headquarters, Gloucester, May 6th.[5]

Great emphasis was placed on the care of the horse and the need to understand the
disposition of the horse. This has been stated succinctly by a more recent authority:

> To the surprise of some, horses have differing qualities, get up to mischief, and are
> reported on their Annual Horse Report. Knowing every horse is as important as
> knowing every rider to ensure that the rider is suited to the horse. Any mismatch is
> quickly discovered with a loose horse and an injured jockey.[6]

Routine inspections at exercises had shown that care of mounts was not always of high
enough standard. Local foraging was variable so that 'neither army rations nor foraging were reliable and horses suffered accordingly'. There was an unavoidable weight
of man and equipment on the horse's back but this was to be restricted 'because over-
loading was causing even more sore backs on the long suffering beasts'. Therefore the

requisite weight was to be 'one quarter of the horse's body weight or 250lb'. Officers were also reminded that some NCOs 'varied in their conscientiousness' and needed to be supervised closely. Directions about stable fatigues were specific:

> Hay that is Dusty or Mouldy should be sprinkled with Water and well shaked up. The Stables to be kept cold & free from any bad smell as nothing more Contributes to the Health of a Horse – when there are not proper air Holes they must be made … The Horses Tails to be Cut, the first of every Month. The Legs are on no account ever to be touched with Scissors. Hand dressing will always clear away the Superfluous Hairs, the Edges of the Ears may occasionally be Clipt, but never inside, the long hair under the Jaws may be Singed. In a Stable without stalls each man to stand by his Horse while Feeding … the Hay well shaked before given. The Horses Cloathes to be kept as Clean as Possible & therefore Washed & Scowered when necessary.

The 1844 Yeomanry Regulations which were 'issued by the government Department connected with yeomanry' were an abridgement of the regulations for regular cavalry. They were more detailed than T. Dicey & Co.'s 1798 county booklet for Northampton but confirmed the recommendations of the earlier plan of exercise. They imposed firm instructions such as the standard system of fines previously mentioned.[7] Much of the 250-page book was taken up with drill procedures, some of them of the familiar 'March!' and 'Halt!' variety, but others a little more exotic, such as 'To Fire a Feu de Joie on Foot' – presumably what is now done by liberated citizens of countries having unseated their dictators. The text then goes on to practical fieldwork against an enemy, as well as 'arrangements on occasions of Riots and General Disturbances'.

Some of the fieldwork required geometric accuracy from the rural Yeomen of scant schooling. One evolution concerns an advance guard which is charged with marking out 'an Alignment', a defence line, the width of the regiment and at an oblique angle between two distant landmarks, say a windmill and a church steeple. NCOs were required to be able to do this. The directions for just the first phase of the 'Alignment', with two riders, 'A' and 'B', give a flavour of the manoeuvres required:

> 'A' chooses one of the objects, say the mill, as his regulating point, and places himself with his side towards it, and his horse's head towards the intended Alignment. 'B' instantly posts himself about fifty yards from 'A', on that side of him which is farthest from the mill, with his horse's head towards the intended Alignment and dresses himself exactly on 'A' and the mill. As soon as he has placed himself correctly as described, he gives the word '*Ready*', upon which they both start, 'A' riding straight forward at a steady canter towards where the head of the Column is to follow, occasionally glancing his eye towards the Steeple; and 'B' riding a certain degree faster so as to keep the mill still exactly in a line with 'A' as he advances, and at the same time preserving his fifty yards distance from his flank …

For review purposes, once a regiment was formed up in line or column, there were twenty-one different movements from the line, such as half turn, change front, invert and retire, plus six movements from close column and seventeen movements from open

Marches from the Right to the Front.

By Threes.

fig. 1

"*Advance by Threes from the Right.*" "*Threes Right.*" The right-hand Three both of the front and rear rank stands fast; the remainder wheel Threes right. (fig. 1.)

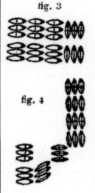

fig. 2

"*March.*" The right-hand Three of the front rank moves straight to the front; its rear-rank Three moves up to it by inclining; the remainder move on and wheel to the left at the same point from which the right-hand Three advanced. (fig. 2)

fig. 3

By Sections of Threes.

"*Advance by Sections of Threes from the Right.*" "*Threes Right.*" The right-hand Three both of the front and rear rank stands fast; the remainder wheel "Threes Right." (fig. 3.)

fig. 4

"*March.*" The leading Three marches straight to the front, followed by its rear rank; the remainder move off their ground in succession; first a front-rank and then a rear-rank Three, alternately, and wheel to the left at the same point from which the leading Three advanced. (fig. 4.)

Two of the drill moves from the 1844 book of instructions.

column, all to be learned and rehearsed to perfection. When it came to action and the command to charge was issued, this followed the set sequence of 'March! Trot! Gallop! Charge! … Walk! Halt!' The vital principle of the charge was that 'it is from uniform velocity of a Line that its greatest effect is derived; it must, therefore, on no account, be so much hurried as to bring up the horses blown, or even distressed to the attack'.

Normally on a route march the speed of advance would be 6mph. In cases of great urgency 8mph might be permitted but only for brief periods. There were four motions of the horse, each with a speed detailed for exercises: the 'Walk' would be at about 4mph; the 'Trot' could be from 7–8½mph; the 'Canter' around 11mph; and the 'Charge' was to be no faster than the speed of the slowest horse and not exceeding a moderate hand gallop. The racecourse or hunting gallop was not contemplated for horses in formation. A ¼-mile distance must be marked out and horses and riders 'habituated' to cover that distance at correct speeds; for instance, the quicker trot would complete the distance in exactly one minute and forty-six seconds, with NCOs' stopwatches to hand! This certainly was precision riding.

No doubt some Yeomen would become a little bored or frustrated with an endless regime of such exercises. And no doubt the men of the Kettering Troop would have been delighted to know that the monotony was to be broken by a royal visit to the burgh. In November 1844 Queen Victoria and her consort, Prince Albert, had been invited to a christening at Burleigh. There was as yet no railway station in Northampton so the royal couple would descend from their train at Weedon and continue by horse carriage, passing through Kettering. It was an opportunity for the Yeomen to don their finery, immaculate scarlet tunics with dark-blue facing, gold epaulets and plentiful gold lace, and the riders' heights enhanced by their bell-top shakos. They would polish their swords and percussion carbines, and diligently 'skower their Horse Cloathes'.

The royals were to change horses at the White Hart Inn before proceeding to Stamford. Captain William Maunsell, commanding the Kettering Troop, waited with civic dignitaries at Market Hill to greet the couple, and it was Lieutenant Booth who would have the honour of commanding the escort through the streets and on towards Stamford. The formation was strictly ordered: an advanced guard of two riders, followed by an NCO; then the advanced party of twelve Yeomen formed in threes; a flanker riding on each side of the lead horses, an officer flanker at each side level with the carriage windows; two more flankers immediately behind the coach; and finally a rear part of twelve, an NCO and two 'whippers in'. At the Market Hill the troop band stood and played the national anthem. Crowds lined the streets and a 17-year-old girl was inspired to poetry:

> On Market Hill our great Yeomanry stood
> To guard Queen Victoria to Weedon in the Wood
> While through the High Street in Ket'ring she rides
> With a thousand spectators arrayed on both sides.

Other county regiments carried out similar colourful engagements. When the commander in the Crimea, Lord Raglan, died, he was afforded a state funeral from a ceremonial barge in Bristol docks to a vault at Badminton. The vanguard of the processions and the guard at the vault were provided by the Yeomanry Cavalry of Gloucestershire and Monmouth, now honoured as the Royal Gloucester Hussars.

Throughout the century Yeomanry troops were being raised or disbanded all over the country. None was more bizarre or remote than the unique Bengal Yeomanry which existed from 1857 to 1861 during the Indian Mutiny. Raised and equipped within a week by Lord Canning, with a strength of 258, and commanded by a Colonel Richardson CB, it consisted of clerks, indigo planters, midshipmen from the P&O line and newly arriving officers not yet appointed. The force took part in fourteen engagements, and at one of these actions, Amorha in March 1858, the British, Sikh and Gurkha troops were at a disadvantage of twelve to one. The insurrectionist army overlapped their front by a mile on either flank. The flanks were guarded by the Bengal Yeomanry and a 'brilliant charge' by the horsemen was an important element in the hard-won victory. The Bengal Yeomanry gained the name of *Shaitan-i-Pultan* – The Devil's Regiment.

The latter part of the century saw measures to tighten organisation and upgrade efficiency in a way commensurate with the development of modern warfare. The issue of breech-loading carbines greatly increased the rapidity of fire and allowed accuracy at targets twice the former distance, up to 200 yards. Independent troops were abolished and the minimum size of a regiment fixed. There would be thirty-six regiments with a total strength of 11,850 officers and men, and Yeomen were signed on for a minimum of three years. Two national inspectors of auxiliary cavalry were also appointed.

In 1893 there was a further reorganisation: formal squadrons were initiated within regiments; regiments would be formed into brigades; a permanent staff of NCOs would function at regimental and squadron level; and there would be 'Trained Yeoman' courses and musketry courses. A Yeoman failing for two years to pass the third-class test at musketry would be struck off the roll. On the other hand, a third-class pass would be rewarded by one extra day's pay of 3*s* 6*d*.

One inspecting staff officer uttered words of ominous and almost prophetic import when assessing a regimental exercise. Reflecting on the First Boer War of 1881, he remarked of the Yeomen:

> The firing was too rapid. There as no attempt at taking aim, the sole object of the men seemed to be to fire off their cartridges as quick as they could. If they were on active service they would soon discover the necessity of husbanding their ammunition … the Yeomanry represent what the Boers did in the Transvaal. The Boers were men who could ride and shoot and had shown England what an extremely effective and valuable force a body of Yeomanry could be, if only they knew how to ride, how to do outpost duty, and, at the same time, if they were good shots.[8]

Some of the Yeomen addressed by this sage would soon learn for themselves just how accurate and elusive the Boers could be. And some would pay a price if they themselves did not attain equal levels of horsemanship and marksmanship, far away from county camps, in the wide open spaces of South Africa.

CHAPTER THREE

BOER WAR OR BORE WAR?
(1899–1902)

The Yeomanry had to wait more than 100 years before experiencing serious combat under fire from an enemy. Even then it did not seem to be much of a war when the civilian Dutch farmers of South Africa's Transvaal and Orange Free State, also known as 'Boers' (the simple Dutch name for 'farmer' which had become transmuted into a national designation), invaded the British-ruled Cape Colony in October 1899, to commence the Second Boer War. There might be a brief chance of cavalry glory in fast, galloping charges before the serried might of the well-trained British infantry ranks crushed those insolent rural oafs.

Trooper Arthur Arnold, a Northamptonshire volunteer, wrote home on 2 March 1900: 'It seems to be the general idea that the war will soon be over. Lord Methuen thinks so.'[1] It proved to be prolonged, embarrassing, frustrating, uncomfortable and boring. Later, Arthur, from a decent Northamptonshire farmstead, commented: 'We have a job to keep free of lice, nearly all of us are as lousy as jays. It is a lousy war … This 22 miles we always have to march in the night and there is no water; when we have to escort the ox convoy we only travel at the rate of two miles an hour, so that it is a very weary march.' No chance for the gallant galloping they had trained so hard for!

Conditions on arrival were not reassuring for healthy young men from the shires. The Royal Gloucester Hussars, no longer in splendid tunics but dressed in khaki, wearing slouch hats and carrying Lee-Metford rifles, were marched from Cape Town piers straight to Maitland Camp. 'The camp was very overcrowded with nine regiments where there was room for only three. Dysentery and enteric fever were rife. Colonel Challoner fell ill and was invalided home. After a fortnight they were glad to get out of that disease-ridden hole.'[2]

To everyone's surprise, at the start of the war 40,000 Boers swooped and laid siege to Kimberley, Ladysmith and Mafeking. The British infantry at last formed line of battle against the evasive farmers who were also impressive hunters and sharpshooters. The Boers' shooting skills, the burning sun and the endless open veldt combined to inflict disastrous defeats on the slow-moving, mechanically drilled British at Stormberg, Magersfontein, Colenso in December 1899 and Spion Kop in January 1900. The blistering sun caused as many casualties as Boer bullets to the bare legs and posteriors of kilted Highlanders, pinned down by superior individual marksmanship, in the open, without shelter or water and unable to move for hours on end.

The world-encircling British Empire reeled in astonishment. South African politician Cecil Rhodes' dream of a British red-coloured strip of territory carrying a railway line from Cape Town to Cairo withered almost overnight. From the British leaders the call went out for mounted troops able to combat the fast-moving Dutch farmers on their Basuto ponies. The regular British cavalry were too few, but there was still the Yeomanry. However, there was another fatal 'but' as the Yeomanry in its official form could not normally serve outside the British Isles. An open clause covering exceptional demands from the sovereign made it possible to call for Yeomen volunteers who would defend the sovereign's lands, but at a distance of thousands of miles across the sea.

In 1900 some 10,000 Yeomen volunteered and were sent to South Africa on service contracts of twelve months. In early 1901 another 17,000 went out to replace or reinforce the previous year's drafts, and again in late 1901 another 7,000 volunteers crossed the sea. After varying fortunes in the nineteenth century, by 1899 some Yeomanry units still existed as fully formed regiments, while others soldiered on as individual squadrons or troops. At the time, the NY formed as the Northampton Squadron under Lord Anally, although some NY volunteers, like Arthur Arnold, were drafted into the neighbouring Royal Bucks Hussars. On 22 January 1900 the *Northampton District Recorder* reported that a Northamptonshire Imperial Yeomanry contingent was leaving for South Africa.

The existing 'regiments' went to South Africa as numbered 'companies' of what was now the 'Imperial Yeomanry', the Bucks providing 37th and 38th companies. The main advantage was that they went as mounted troops, able to shoot from the saddle or dismounted in infantry form. Most units stayed with the traditional rifle or carbine, pistol and sword; however, the Queen's Own Worcestershire Hussars had 2lb and 3lb guns, which were the personal property of Lord Plymouth and their use of ammunition in action had to be funded privately.

After the initial battle shocks, and as increasing numbers of imperial troops poured in from Britain, Canada and Australia, the Boers resorted to tactics of ghosting in rapidly from the seemingly boundless spaces of low hills and parched

Lord Anally, Pytchley Hunt Master and reforming colonel, *c.*1900. *(Kind permission of Northampton Art Gallery)*

desert, striking where least expected and then disappearing. As Arthur Arnold saw it in August 1900:

> They attacked the grazing guard the other side of town, killing one man. The next day a convoy came in from Kroonstad – the enemy tried hard to capture it but it managed to drive them off. A section of the 38th Battery R.H.A. was nearly captured on July 3rd. They [the Boers] crept up close to them disguised in khaki helmets and blue overcoats. The 38th had the Major and Lieutenant killed, a Captain wounded, beside fifteen of the men killed, wounded and missing. If it had not been for the Yeomanry coming up in the nick of time, they would all have been captured.

The military system of the Boers, if it could be called that, was similar to the British Yeomanry formations. The Boer states had only trained artillerymen and mounted police, and beyond that their 'commandos' consisted mainly of farmers who could bring their own horses to the battle. In normal life the farmers relied on their own hunting and tracking skills to provide meat for the family. One German observer noted that 'each man learned to study the country, avail himself of cover in order to get within effective range of his adversary [animal or human], and only to fire when success was certain, but to fly quickly from danger'.[3]

Probably the first substantial opportunity for Yeomanry action came near the isolated town of Boshof on 5 April 1900. Lord Methuen commanded the 9th Infantry Brigade (Yorkshire Light Infantry, Northampton Regiment, Northumberland Fusiliers and North Lancashire Regiment) and was able to call on some 500 Imperial Yeomanry troops under Lord Chesham. Trooper Tudor Crosthwaite of 39th (Berkshire) Company recalled with a sense of thrill: 'I was having a wash (a rare event) outside the camp when I heard the "boot and saddle" call, just got to camp in time to get on the horse as the column of Yeomanry mounted rifles moved off.'[4]

British colonial expansion was watched with apprehension by other ambitious nations. On the mainland of Europe there was much sympathy for the Boers and not only on the part of the 'High Dutch' in the Netherlands. A number of French volunteers served with the Boers and one of them was commanding the Boer force near Boshof. President Kruger had just promoted Colonel the Count de Villebois Mareuil to general. De Villebois Mareuil was a notable French strategist with battle experience in Cochin China and in France itself against the Germans, and had been awarded the Legion of Honour for his exploits. Like other French sympathisers, he had reached the Transvaal via Madagascar and Mozambique, and took charge of a raiding commando.

After the Boshof battle, Yeomen of the Berkshires found on his body his complete plan to storm the camp at Boshof, ride on to the Modder River and destroy the vital bridge there, and then afterwards to vanish into the veldt. He had anticipated facing only infantry, artillery and other grounded troops, which were prime victims for a commando raid appearing suddenly and swiftly out of the unguarded distances, and had not counted on a British mounted unit being in the vicinity. De Villebois Mareuil's force consisted of only 100 men, a small number in comparison to other wars but a large and dangerous group when let loose among the kopjes, the relativity small but tactically formidable hills. These are scattered over the arid South African

Boer War – the Queen's Own Dorset Yeomanry lead advance into Johannesburg. *(Keep Museum, Dorset Yeo)*

countryside in total disorder and had not yet been adequately mapped. But as the enthusiastic, close-formed Boer commando hit the camp it gave the hard-riding Yeomanry an opportunity to surround and surprise them.

Trooper Crossthwaite had a hectic ride of 7 miles 'to a place called Kokkfontein [Koffyfontein] when we, immediately, gave the gentlemen our attention'. For troopers, some of whom had hunted over verdant pastures such as the Althorp estate, it was not easy going. Trooper Evans, rubbing bruised limbs, jotted down:

> I had my first fall. My company was galloping across the plain to head off the party of Boers when one of the horses put his foot in a hole – the veldt is full of holes – and over he went. I turned back to give the chap a hand but as he did not happen to want any help I galloped after my company again. I had just got up to racing speed again when my horse put his foot into a 2 foot deep hole, and over we rolled. I got up with only a scratched nose and bruised thumb. Lucky wasn't I, considering the pace I was going? Quite a dozen or more of our fellows had the same mishap during that day.

Trooper the Hon. Sidney Peel observed that 'a native-born pony will avoid any dark or suspicious-looking spot as by instinct, and will even pass a hole in a moment without pressure of rein or leg, but an English horse, fresh from smooth pastures or hard roads, will put his nose in the air and give his rider tumble after tumble'. So a rider must look out sharply and continually for holes 'which is not consistent with good scouting'. Trooper Evans later noted that 'we killed eighteen horses with over-riding and only two horses wounded [by enemy fire]. My horse was completely done and I could only get a walk out of him.' In retrospect this may seem cruel but the Boers had already gained a reputation for hard and skilful riding across the terrible terrain. If the Yeomanry were to encircle and cut off such a mobile force, there was no time to halt for a stirrup cup or to observe the normal rules for followers of the Pytchley Hunt.

The British force which quickly assembled at Boshof was overwhelming, comprising companies of the Berks, the Bucks, the Oxfords, the Sherwood (Rangers) and the Yorkshire Yeomanry under Lord Chesham, and the Kimberley Mounted Rifles (a South African version of the Yeomanry) all riding hard, with artillery guns following up. Seeing the British reaction, the Boers had taken up a strong position among the projecting rocks of a kopje where the flanking companies surrounded them. The leading horsemen, about twenty or so, came upon the hidden Boers almost by accident and had to dismount and go to ground under heavy fire, whilst the flanking movement continued. An officer was killed and four men wounded. Other riders settled on two smaller kopjes and exchanged fire at about 600 yards whilst the Kimberley men brought up a Maxim gun.

One trooper observed how the enemy were unable to escape as they had left their horses grazing down on the plain. 'Every time they tried to catch them we bowled them over with rifle shots'. Sergeant Duck, sitting in support and writing as he watched, noted: 'we have run down a party of Boers and Rebels, and like shooting rabbits in England, they have gone to ground.' As the main body of Yeomanry dismounted and moved to attack they came under heavy rifle fire, which became very accurate at about 150 yards' range. Major Lawson, commanding the attack, had some difficulty in restraining what were still rather novice soldiers, for they were moving forward too eagerly and exposing themselves to possible heavy casualties.

Lawson reported: 'when closing in upon the top of the kopje, our men, cheering wildly, were advancing with fixed bayonets when the Boers hoisted a white flag.' Unfortunately the firing continued and Captain Williams, 'who unfortunately exposed himself too early', was killed and others wounded. De Villebois Mareuil had apparently said that he would fight to the death and was indeed killed towards the end of the action. This led to the hoisting of the white flag without a central commander to co-ordinate the surrender.

As the attackers counted the prisoners they were astonished to find that out of about a hundred apparent Boers, thirty-two were volunteers from Holland, twenty-nine Frenchmen, a Russian or two, a variety of other Europeans and only nine local Free State Boers, which revealed the strength of European opposition to British colonial expansion. There was one English rebel, Coleman, 'a citizen of Boshof'. The Boer commandos said that, once surrounded, they had wanted to surrender without firing but their French commander, who more than anyone must have realised the uselessness of resistance, had insisted on maintaining a hopeless fight.

There was opportunity for some grim humour. One 'vivacious little fellow, a Corsican named Antonio', asked his captor Sydney Peel if he might be employed as an orderly in an English hospital. Peel told him that he was much more likely to spend time 'upon an island not unfamiliar to his greatest compatriot'. St Helena, with its memories of Napoleon Bonaparte, was indeed one of the convenient locations to which increasing numbers of Boer prisoners were shipped for the duration.

The Yeomanry in general were not yet inured to death and bereavement. Tough Sergeant Duck watched as the Red Cross vans came in to camp and shuddered:

Here comes the poor sergeant's body; poor fellow! The bullet entered his mouth, turned and came out of his forehead. Following him come the two Lieutenants. The bodies look too dreadful. It makes your heart race to see about a dozen dead bodies who only a little while ago were in strength and health. Nearly all the bullets they were using are the prohibited ones – explosive and soft noses. I have one of their bandoliers and it is nearly full of them.

Trooper Tudor Crossthwaite pondered that charging the Boer with the bayonet was 'quite an unnecessary proceeding and costing us five men', whereas if the artillery had been left to get on with the job the Boer group would have been wiped out with fewer casualties. There was sadness as 'the same evening we buried friend and foe alike, with military honours in a melancholy little graveyard and the bugles sounded the Last Post over those who sleep there unforgotten'.

It seemed then as though the gods of war intended to make a mockery of the puny human beings with their Maxim guns and Lee-Metford rifles. Tudor Crossthwaite quailed as they rode home 'in the most awful thunderstorm, thunder, lightning, moon, stars, rain and rainbow all at once. We lost our way, the darkness succeeding, the lightning indescribable and the depth of water we rode in must have been a foot.' Sydney Peel felt that 'the crashing thunder so contemptuously surpassed the petty noises of our puny fight, the vivid lighting and drenching rain were awe-inspiring in the extreme'. Sergeant Duck agreed: '… it was pitch dark and it thundered and lightened awfully. It was one perpetual flame of forked lighting. We were told if we liked we could go into town, knock anybody up and demand a bed. So we commandeered the first house we came to. 'Twas an empty house so we made a large fire and dried our clothes.'

There was no rest as Sergeant Duck 'started in the morning again at 4.30. The rain had been coming down in torrents all night.' Although the main body of enemy had been surrounded and dealt with, there were other out-riders to be chased. Duck's section came to a farm where the attackers had made their camp for the night before battle as the owner of the farm was 'a leader of the gang'. Duck's men contented themselves by 'stripping his farm of young potatoes, geese, fowls, ducks, marrows, etc. … In a pit we found thousands of rounds of ammunition. All the bullets' ends had been poisoned.'

The fight at Boshof may have been minor in relation to other battles just fourteen years later, but it was a larger affair than most of the action which Yeomen would experience during the rest of the war in South Africa. The more the Boers were ousted in larger skirmishes, the more they resorted to wider-reaching and unexpected attacks of the commando type, often appearing many miles, even hundreds of miles, behind British spearheads. For the slowly advancing British troops this meant months of frustration, minor injuries and discomfort with little of the reputed glory of the light cavalry era.

The overall experience is well illustrated in the letters which Trooper Arthur Arnold wrote home to family at Deenethorpe in Northamptonshire, and extracts from some of those letters paint a clear picture of a plodding advance. He commenced his letters when, like many young men who otherwise would never have travelled to foreign climes, he started his great adventure with the sea voyage to Cape Town:[5]

S.S. 'Norman',
Sunday, February 18th, 1900

My dear sister,

I have got nothing to do so I thought I would just sit down and write a few lines … We got to Madeira on Thursday Feb 14th. It is a beautiful little town. It was quite a change to see everything looking green.

We had divine service this morning on the boat deck. The service was taken by Lord [Colonel] Chesham. It was only a short one because his Lordship did not give a sermon. As soon as the service was over a lot of us had to go and be vaccinated. It is compulsory. I can just begin to feel mine paining me, I expect we shall have to be inoculated next.

It is very hot now. We do all our drills and knock about in shirt sleeves, overalls and canvas shoes.

One of our men broke his leg in the Bay of Biscay so they put him ashore in Madeira as it was no use going to South Africa with a broken leg. We go about four hundred miles in twenty four hours now.

With best love to all,
Arthur

—ⱮⱮ—

S.S. 'Dictator'
Cape Town,
March 2nd, 1900

My dear sister,

We arrived on Wednesday morning. Had us up at three. Got all our things on the quay, baggage, ammunition, and everything for the campaign. Everybody got as black as sweeps as they were coaling at the time. Four o'clock we received orders to get everything back on the 'Norman' as we were to go to East London. Got back on board. Stayed all night.

Took us for a march in the morning and promised us leave in Cape Town. When we got back, orders for us to go on the 'Dictator' as the 'Norman' does not leave here until Saturday. Scores of ships in harbour, loaded with soldiers, horses, mules, stores, etc for the front. The 'Majestic' has just come in with the 17th Lancers.

We had leave last night to go into Cape Town. Everybody was rejoicing at the relief of Kimberley and Ladysmith. Thousands of people marching through the town singing. Flags flying everywhere, such a sight as never seen before.

I am in good health and hope you are all the same at home.

Your loving brother,
Arthur

P.S. It seems to be the general idea that the war will soon be over.

Queenstown Camp,
March 9th, 1900

My dear sister,

We got to East London on Sunday night. Had a busy time getting ready to go off by train. Went at twelve o'clock and did not arrive in Queenstown until 7 o'clock the next morning, being on the train nineteen hours without getting out.

We got our horses on Wednesday. They are most of them Basuto ponies, not very big, but seem active and wiry. Reveille goes at five in the morning. Then we feed and water the horses. We have fifteen men in our tent so we are packed like sardines. We get fresh meat every day but we have to kill our own. It makes some of the best soup I have ever tasted.

There are a lot of rebels in this district. All the night sentries are warned that if they are found asleep at their post they will be shot. We are not allowed in town. Where we are camped is on the veldt, surrounded by kopjes. It is no wonder the Boers take a lot of shifting off them. It is sandy soil and very dry. It is very hot in daytime. We all sleep with 100 rounds of ball cartridges under our heads and a rifle at our feet. I think some of us will have to escort a baggage train. There will be about 200 wagons in it, with sixteen oxen to each, so it should reach a long way.

We get newspapers but none of us has yet had a letter from home. There are thousands of locusts. Sometimes the air is almost black with them while the ground is covered. I have not seen any wild animals yet but hear them in the night.

Just remember me to all my friends.

Your loving brother
Arthur

—𝑚—

Hoopstad,
Saturday, May 20th, 1900

Dear father,

Just a few lines to let you know how I am getting on. We started from Boshof on Monday and marched to Driefontein (15 miles), then 15 miles the next day. Then on Wednesday we started three o'clock in the morning. Marched 15 miles then rested until half past six then started off again. It was twenty-four miles we marched in the night and for nineteen miles there was no water to drink.

I don't think the war will last much longer as all the Free Staters are bringing in their arms, all sorts from muzzle loaders to the best Mauser rifles. Hoopstad is a small town and all the country is flat. We have seized a lot of cattle and horses, but do not allow looting.

We had a sergeant die last week with fever, but I keep in very good health, but have a job to keep free of lice, nearly all of us are lousy as jays.

I hope that you will have a good summer and shall not be surprised if I am home for the harvest.

Your affectionate son,
Arthur

—⁂—

Heilbron
August 17th, 1900

My dear sister,

We have had a pretty rough time of it since I last wrote. While we were at Lindley it was besieged by the Boers under General De Wet. Had a job to keep them out. They attacked the Yorkshire picquet, got close to them but they managed to drive them off although they lost a lot of men – 14 men killed and wounded. The Yeomanry got there just in time to save them.

A section of the 38th Battery R.H.A. was nearly captured in July 3rd. They crept up close to them disguised in khaki helmets and blue overcoats. Prince Alfred's Guards ran away when they saw them and if it had not been for the Yeomanry coming up in the nick of time they would have been captured.

On July 13th we were sent out to repair telegraph lines. The officer in command of our troop made a great mistake and led thirty of our troop to attack a very steep kopje with 200 Boers on it. We got within 100 yards of it before we had the order to retire. Of our thirty men there were three killed, five wounded and three taken prisoner, beside the officer wounded in the legs.

On Monday July 23rd we looted two farms. I got a goose, some rice, flour, butter, jam and onions. On the Sunday we had to climb up a mountain which took us two hours to get to the top. When we got there we could see four Boer laagers a few miles off. Marched fifteen miles that day. I had to do it on Shanks's pony [walking] as they shot up five grazing horses the day before, mine amongst them.

We all want new clothes now. Some of the men haven't got a whole shirt to their backs while their breeches and jackets are all holes. The regulars had winter clothing weeks ago but the Imperial Yeomanry have had to manage without. Nearly everybody thought the war would be over now but as soon as we have smashed one lot of Boers up, there is another lot springs up somewhere else. The Boers never make a stand now.

I must conclude with best love to all, hoping that you will have a good harvest on the farm.

Your loving brother,
Arthur

—⁂—

Mafeking,
September 10th, 1900

My dear Mary,

Just to let you know how I have been getting on lately. We let Heilbron on 21st August for Kroonstad, got here on the 24th, got new clothing here, but did not find any letters, only some tobacco and a pipe from Neville Hepburn.

About two hundred of us went out on a patrol on Sunday 2nd under Major Rimington after De Wet who had blown the railway line up; but did not find him. Burned a farm down where he had been, got back on Monday morning two o'clock. Had orders to go to Mafeking to join [General] Lord Methuen. Started on Thursday morning. We rode on cattle trucks passed through Bloemfontein – got to Mafeking Sunday afternoon. Found Lord Methuen had gone and that our letters had been sent on to Krugersdorp.

We are busy today getting remounts and start after Methuen tomorrow morning, hoping that we catch him so that I can get my letters. I am in first rate health, now weigh thirteen stones all but a lb, more than two stones heavier than when I came out. A lot of the Yeomanry are joining the Police [on expiry of their twelve months' service].

I expect you have finished harvest by now. Hope you had a good time. Mafeking is not a very big place. It is very flat all round. I expect that was what enabled BP [Baden Powell] to hold out so long.

Just remember me to all enquiring friends,

Your loving brother,
Arthur

—w—

Mafeking,
January 1st, 1901

My dear sister,

I was very pleased to get a letter from Fred dated Nov. 22nd. Today, we have two weeks mail. I had three letters, one from Aunt Jennie who sent me a box of Congleton ginger-bread. It is the first parcel I have received although I know several have been sent out.

We have been doing garrison duty at Lichtenburg. On Christmas Eve we had a bottle of champagne to every three men, and some cake, and had a very good concert in the Dutch church. Christmas Day I was on guard at night but we had a quart of stout each and a plum pudding each.

On Saturday we had orders to pack up and come to Mafeking. It was one of the wettest nights I have been in yet. It simply poured. We halted at half past ten at night, but didn't get our blankets and waterproof sheets off the wagons because we had to start again at two o'clock in the morning. So we just lay down, rather sat down, on our saddles in our cloaks and made the best of it. These twenty-two miles we have to march through the night always because there is no water. When we have to escort the ox convoy we only travel at the rate of two miles an hour.

We are waiting for orders. Think we are going down country to Vriburg after a commando named De Burr. There doesn't seem much chance of us being home for some time yet. Think it is about time they sent some of the Regular Troops who are messing about in barracks at home, out to relieve us. We have just completed our twelve months service the time we signed on for.

I was sorry to hear that father is ailing and hope by this time he is much better.

Your affectionate brother,
Arthur

—m—

Lilliefontein,
February 7th, 1901

My dear Mary,

I have just received a letter from you dated Oct. 29th. On Sunday we got to a place where I was hit a few weeks before. Had a sharp go again and 8 Bushmen and New Zealanders were wounded and one or two have died since. The next day we had a lot of sniping and a few horses shot.

This morning we went out commandeering and had a lot of sniping from the Boers. We get used to being shot at now, although there are not the half of us that there were at first, I think we are better now than the full squadron used to be.

You seem to be having a gay time at Deenethorpe this Christmas, having dances, taking part in entertainments, etc. I shall be left in the lurch when I come back but I suppose the khaki uniform will help me out!! It is rumoured we shall be on our way home in March but I have heard these tales so often … ???

Your affectionate brother,
Arthur

—m—

Warrenton,
March 27th, 1901

My dear sister,

Well, we have not done much except to cross the river which was a big job, it has been very wet and the Vaal was too swollen to ford. We had to bring all the wagons across by train and then lead the horses across the temporary railway bridge. We expect to move from here tomorrow and it is rumoured this will be our last trek.

There are about a hundred of the New Yeomanry here [1901 draft]. About a dozen of our troopers and NCOs have got commissions in the New Yeomanry. I could have had one if I applied. But it meant staying out for another twelve months. The officers' pay is 15/6 a day but I should have had to keep a servant and pay a share of the mess.

We haven't got last week's mail yet. The 'Norman Castle' broke down so that they have been delayed.

Your affectionate brother,
Arthur

—⁂—

Doornfontein,
April 18th, 1901

My dear sister,

At last I think we are coming home, for it has been given out in Orders that the old Yeomanry are to be broken up today. Lord Methuen thanked us for our good service and said we had marched 2,900 miles. This doesn't include the hundreds of miles we have done on little expeditions.

We have got a full squadron of New Yeomanry here now – rather a rough lot, very different from the old Yeomanry as hardly any of them can ride. Myself and several others have been told to teach them how to ride. The Captain calls them his 'Freaks'.

Expect to rail at the end of this month or the beginning of the next so you needn't write again.

Your loving brother,
Arthur

—⁂—

Perhaps Arthur was a little harsh for the 'New Yeomanry' regiments eventually fought well. In an epic convoy-guarding trek, Lieutenant English of the 2nd Scottish Horse led the fight against overwhelming odds and was awarded the Victoria Cross. Generally, on return, what Arthur called the 'Old Yeomanry' were received as heroes.

Judgements have been more severe in recent time with special contumely reserved for the concentration camps in which families of Boers were confined as the British tried to cut off the Boers' bases, their family farms. Some of the reaction is coloured by parallels drawn with the later concentration camps of the Nazi regime, although the Boer War type were not intended to inflict suffering on the incarcerated families.

What is also forgotten is that Boer women were just as capable as their men at shooting and then retreating into civilian status. Sergeant George Harris later attested to this fact:

They approached a big farm when about thirty rifle shots came from one of the farmhouses ... Before they could fire [their 7-pounder gun] a white flag appeared at the window and a bunch of women and children walked out. The officer asked the women where the men were and got the answer 'gone to the hills to fight' ... He ordered the house to be searched and under the floorboards discovered a dump of rifles and ammunition. It had been the women who had fired on the patrol.

When accused, the 'matriarch of the house' became so violent that, after she had knocked the officer down, Sergeant Harris' men had to tie her hands and ankles to get her into a waiting wagon.[6]

Finally, spare a thought for the horses! The Army Remount Depot in peacetime had the task of finding 2,500 horses a year. According to one source, during the Second Boer War they provided 518,794 mounts in South Africa, and of these 13,144 died on shipboard before arriving, while 347,007 were registered as 'expended during the campaign'.[7]

CHAPTER FOUR

FORMING THE FIGHTING FORCE
(1902–1914)

For the Northamptonshire Yeomanry 1902 seemed almost to be a repeat of 1794. At both dates there was an Earl Spencer who hunted with the Pytchley, chasing foxes across the large Althorp estates. Both held more than one high government office, both served as First Lord of the Admiralty, both had influence at court and both were largely responsible for the founding or re-forming of the county Yeomanry regiment as colonel or honorary colonel.

However, in other ways they were not alike. George John, 2nd Earl Spencer, appears to have been a quiet, almost bookish man, while John, the 5th Earl Spencer, was an extrovert, an 'icon' or 'celebrity' of the time, to use modern parlance. To begin with John Poyntz Spencer, the 5th Earl, sported a voluminous red beard and quickly became known as 'the Red Earl'. One particular event sealed his celebrity status: in 1876 an outstanding woman celebrity, the Empress Elisabeth of Austria, familiarly known as 'Sissi', decided to make a hunting trip to England. Famous at the time for her beauty and tragic story, Sissi has since been featured in film, literature, opera and ballet. She rented a house in Northamptonshire and, from the hunting point of view, was hosted by the Red Earl. The image of the Red Earl with his flowing beard, hunting the fox in the company of the romantic Sissi, caught the nation's imagination.

However, the Red Earl was much more than an idle hunting squire; for instance, he was credited with introducing barbed wire into Britain. Barbed wire had been patented in the USA in 1867 and 1874 and was used in the Boer War, particularly for the construction of the infamous concentration camps for civilians. In a few years' time the Red Earl's newly reconstituted Northamptonshire Yeomanry, like so many more, would learn the bitter lessons of charging barbed-wire entanglements backed by machine-gun fire. The 5th Earl also served twice for long periods as Lord Lieutenant of Ireland at critical stages of the painful progress towards independence of the southern Irish counties.[1]

Now in 1902, as other county Yeomanry returning from the Boer War re-formed their regiments for peacetime training, Earl Spencer wrote to the king offering to raise a Northamptonshire regiment after more than seventy years of operating as independent squadrons or troops. He also requested permission to use the king's own badge, the 'White Horse of Hanover', as the regimental badge. The requests were granted, effective 21 February 1902. Due to the fact that there had not been a continuous regiment operating during those years, 1902 became the date for calculating the seniority of the regiment.

John Poyntz, 5th Earl Spencer, reformed NY in 1902. *(Courtesy of Charles, 9th Earl Spencer)*

THE IMPERIAL YEOMANRY FOR NORTHAMPTONSHIRE.

Since the sanction of the King has been received for the formation of an Imperial Yeomanry Regiment for Northamptonshire the necessary steps have been taken to arrange for the enlistment of intending recruits and for the officering of the regiment. We understand that Lord Annaly will be the commanding officer, and commanding each of the four squadrons will be Captain Wickham, of Barnwell, late of the Scots Greys, whose headquarters will be at Peterborough; Captain Gordon Renton, of Guilsborough, late of the 7th Lancers, headquarters Northampton; Major Jenkinson, Lamport, late of the Derbyshire Regiment, headquarters Kettering; and Captain Leslie Renton, of Guilsborough, late of the Scots Greys, headquarters Daventry.

Recruiting is to begin at once, and the full strength of the regiment will be about 600, including about 120 men who will be transferred from the 3rd Squadron of the Royal Bucks Hussars. The headquarters of the regiment will be at Northampton, and this year's training will probably take place in Althorp Park.

Northampton newspaper report, 1902. *(Chronicle & Echo)*

This meant that it was now junior to other Yeomanry regiments which were founded later than 1794 but had maintained a continuous regimental structure throughout.

Following on from the Boer War title the Yeomanry regiments were now designated 'Imperial Yeomanry' and the 'IY' was incorporated in cap badges. The NY full dress uniform was now of a dragoon pattern, dark blue with light-blue facings and a white metal dragoon helmet with a light-blue and white plume. The service dress was khaki with light-blue facings. Other county regiments were also re-forming and updating their uniforms: the County of London Yeomanry raised an entire regiment of expatriates nicknamed 'The Colonials', the five squadrons each recruited from different country or continent areas, namely Asians, Americans, Australians, Africans and New Zealanders.

Northamptonshire newspapers were now announcing:

THE IMPERIAL YEOMANRY FOR NORTHAMPTONSHIRE

Since the sanction of the King has been received for the formation of an Imperial Yeomanry Regiment for Northamptonshire the necessary steps have been taken to arrange for the enlistment of intending recruits and for the officering of the regiment. We understand that Lord Annaly will be the commanding officer and commanding each squadron will be Captain Wickham, of Barnwell, late of the Scots Greys, whose headquarters will be at Peterborough; Captain Gordon Renton, of Guilsborough, late of the 7th Lancers, headquarters Northampton; Major Jenkinson, Lamport, late of the Derbyshire Regiment, headquarters Kettering; and Captain Leslie Renton, of Guilsborough, late of the Scots Greys, headquarters Daventry.

Recruiting is to begin at once and the full strength of the regiment will be about 600, including about 120 men who will be transferred from the 3rd Squadron of the Royal Bucks Hussars. The headquarters of the regiment will be at Northampton, and this year's training will probably take place in Althorp Park.

Luke White, 3rd Baron Annaly, belonged to the true Yeomanry officer tradition of hard-hunting countrymen, being at the time Master of the Pytchley Hunt. He had commanded the Northampton Squadron attached to the Royal Bucks Hussars, and among the men transferring to the new Northamptonshire Imperial Yeomanry was Trooper Arthur Arnold, the letter writer of the Boer War. Lord Annaly became lieutenant colonel commanding, with the Red Earl as honorary colonel.

The existence of the Peterborough Squadron reflects changing history. In later times Peterborough was associated with Huntingdonshire and Cambridgeshire, but in 1902 the soke of Peterborough was a separate administrative entity, although it was regarded as within the geographical county of Northampton and also part of the Northampton parliamentary county. The Peterborough Squadron continued within the regiment until 1914, its headquarters in the High Street of Peterborough and its horses stabled in Hodgson's Repositories.

Changing times and high recruiting targets meant that, in contrast to the initial recruiting of farmers and smallholders in 1794, the Yeomanry had to make up numbers with some troopers who had never ridden a horse before, much less owned one. They had to

Boer War – Lord Roberts with Yeomanry escort. *(Keep Museum, Dorset Yeo)*

be trained in the elementary tasks of riding and horse care before moving on to the intricate manoeuvres required of mounted dragoons, including the ability to school and ride a horse whilst firing a gun past the horse's ears. Arthur Arnold and other 'Old Yeomanry' from South Africa were involved in instructing this novice 'New Yeomanry'.

One of the learners was George Dixon of the Clipston Troop, C Squadron. He was deeply impressed when he was drilled by 'SSM Kelley of Kettering, a regular soldier with a voice equalling his stature – he must have weighed twenty stone. It was said of him that, in the South African war, he had two Boers on his lance at the same time.' Whether this bloodthirsty tale was mere old soldier's exaggeration or not, George was in awe of the squadron sergeant major (SSM). However, he found the officers like Lieutenant Wartnaby friendly, and every Good Friday the troop members were invited to Major Cazenove's house at Cottesbrooke 'where we had beer, bread and cheese, after tying up our horses'.[2]

Training was difficult for the recruits unused to the rigours of riding a horse and George Dixon wryly commented:

> We were RAW recruits in more ways than one: the military saddles were very hard, but we soon got accustomed to them.
>
> I remember my first camp, I had not been in the saddle for so long a stretch before and I was feeling somewhat sore. The SSM came alongside me and yelled 'Sit up, man. You've got the Dome of St Paul's on your back'. I, being raw at both ends, answered back 'Do you think so!' I do not remember his exact answer, including words I had never heard before, but it did not sound complimentary. I was frightened to death

every time I met him but I have no doubt that he forgot it immediately. I have no doubt it was his and Lieut. Wartnaby's training which made us the very proficient troop which we became.

Dixon was soon able to laugh at other new recruits' foibles. They had become skilled at numbering off, 1, 2, 3, 4, 5 and so on, as fast as machine-gun fire along the line, and on one occasion a new recruit was inserted into the line and the SSM gave the order 'Number'. The numbers shot along the line … 6, 7, 8, but when number 9 was reached the new recruit yelled '9, 10, 11, 12' and went on counting until the SSM's greater shout silenced him. Surprisingly 'SSM Kelley told him in a fatherly way where he had gone wrong'. George was pleased with his blue walking-out uniform, complete with stick and spurs. 'All the girls thought how smart we were, at least that is what WE thought and hoped they would be thinking.'

Among fit and active young men there was also the relief after drill of 'horsing around'. On one occasion after returning to camp, a soldier placed a bottle of beer under his bed and went to sleep. Another lad emptied the beer and replaced it with sheep dip, assuming that the soldier would notice the very different smell. However, the man, apparently very thirsty, woke, grabbed the bottle and took a big swig before anyone could move. He was quite ill for a time but recovered and no lasting harm was done. Nobody owned up to the trick and nobody bothered very much to find out: worse things happened in war.

Worcestershire enacters in red and white tunics hold carbines and sabre. *(Worcs enacters)*

As predicted by the newspapers, the first camp of the regiment was held at Althorp Park in June 1902 and 350 men attended. If some of the more humble troopers were impressed by their surroundings and by the imposing full-dress senior officers like Earl Spencer and Lord Annaly, they were even more overawed to know that their great parade would be inspected by none other than Field Marshal Frederick Sleigh Roberts, 1st Earl of Kandahar, Pretoria and Waterford. Roberts has been called 'perhaps the ablest British field commander since Wellington' having commanded successfully in a number of countries in a long career.[3] He captured Kabul in 1879 and commanded the legendary march from Kabul to Kandahar the following year, while in South Africa he had captured the capitals of both the Transvaal and the Orange Free State. At the same time he was possibly the most popular and trusted senior commander of British armies of all time and was known to the troops simply as 'Bobs'. The feelings of veterans like Arthur Arnold, who had served in South Africa, can well be imagined.

Until the 1902 camp the Yeomanry had been able to hold peacetime camps, which were as much leisure and sporting events as military exercises. Concepts of war had made it possible still to glory in splendid parades, wearing colourful uniforms and carrying out drills which did not always keep pace with reality. The Second Boer War had radically changed serious soldiers' attitudes as the realities of the well-aimed bullet at long range (and Earl Spencer's barbed wire) began to threaten the reliance on sword, sabre or lance. The 1902 camp was still a holiday adventure for most of the troopers, but for officers there were questions to be answered about the tactics and

At a pre-war camp, officers now wearing uniforms appropriate to a European war. *(NYA)*

formations of the future. During the camp at Althorp an excited post corporal delivered a telegram to Lord Roberts from Lord Kitchener stating that the peace treaty to end the Second Boer War had now been signed at Vereeniging. The war had ended but its tactical implications had not.

Camps continued regularly and in 1903 Bertie Taylor, aged 9, went with two other boys into the camp and managed to secure a 'contract' to collect rubbish at 1*d* per boy per day. Unfortunately bad weather and floods terminated the camp after only nine days, so Bertie's profit was only 9*d*; nevertheless, he was so thrilled that he vowed to join up when old enough and eventually became a hero of the Battle of Arras in 1917. It was not all easy fun with horses plunging around when handled without due skill and care. 'Jockey' Wilson was a blacksmith's son at Brington (near Althorp) whose papers of apprenticeship had been signed by the Red Earl. He enthusiastically attended camps at Althorp and Felixstowe but was appalled when another trooper was killed at Althorp as his horse galloped full tilt into a tree.

The time for great changes was not quite upon them and training continued mainly at troop level according to the timetables convenient in the locality, with a lessening of parades during harvest, for example. When the entire regiment got together its list of camps sounded like a roll call of ancestral estates: Althorp, Milton Park, Castle Ashby, Rockingham Castle, Boughton Park.

In 1906 Lieutenant General Sir Ian Hamilton, who was later to command Yeomanry regiments at Gallipoli, inspected annual camps and was impressed. He expressed:

> … his satisfaction at their high level of efficiency. The officers belong to a class fond of energetic country pursuits, they are certainly above average. The NCOs and men ride boldly and well, half of them own their own horses which are of excellent quality. Nothing could be better than the physique of all ranks … his only regret is he had no opportunity of leading such a fine body of men on active service.

Ominous last words when Yeomanry under Hamilton were to suffer heavy casualties as foot soldiers in the costly Gallipoli landings.[4]

In 1907, whilst Secretary of State for War, Lord Haldane pondered momentous changes to the Yeomanry, and the Northamptonshire Yeomanry camp took on a jollier note than previously. For the Rockingham Castle rendezvous a regimental band had been formed and *John Peel* had been selected as the marching song; it was a popular choice. Troopers particularly enjoyed bellowing out loudly the last verse:

> Then here's to John Peel with my heart and soul,
> Come fill, fill to him another strong bowl.

It is not recorded what Master of the Hunt Lord Annaly thought of the choice, for John Peel (who was only 17 in 1794) was not a member of the Pytchley by any means, and did not wear the 'Pink'. His dress is said to have been a drab grey coat, a choker tie, a top hat and shoes with only one spur. He would not have qualified for the Yeomanry as his horse 'Dunny', at 14.3 hands high, was too small for regimental requirements. However, Dunny had one qualification which some troopers might have envied: he had been trained to 'kneel like a camel' so that John Peel, after many strong bowls, as was his wont, might mount and dismount without accident.

It was probably not the choice of *John Peel* as marching song which prompted Lord Annaly's retirement as commanding officer after long service. He was replaced at the Rockingham Castle camp by Lieutenant Colonel Eyre Coote. Future camps would be organised not only in accordance with the wishes of a new CO but also under new conditions for the entire British Army now being presented to the king and Parliament. The independent initiatives of the past 114 years would be subsumed into the grand design of the Territorial Force.

In 1906 Sir Henry Campbell-Bannerman's Liberal party won a landslide victory at the general election, giving them great freedom of action. Richard Burdon Haldane, later Lord Haldane (1911), was appointed Secretary for War and held the post through to 1912, and is regarded as one of the great military reformers. Aware of the possibility of a war on the European Continent, he established the framework for the British Expeditionary Force (BEF) and set up the Imperial General Staff. Among his other innovations was an Advisory Committee for Aeronautics which continued until the 1970s and gave British science a basis for developing aircraft, both for war and civil use.

Haldane's Territorial and Reserve Forces Act of 1907, becoming effective through 1908, was of major interest to the Yeomanry. At the local level this established county Yeomanry regiments, each administered by a county association under the leadership of the Lord Lieutenant. These would supply the mounted units to complement the infantry volunteer regiments. Soldiers were not compelled to serve overseas but could volunteer for overseas service, and efforts were made to persuade them to volunteer ready for any future conflict. In the case of Northamptonshire the Lord Lieutenant was the Red Earl, and in 1908 he was succeeded in that role by Charles Robert Spencer, who later became the 6th Earl.

The newly established fifty-four regiments of mounted Yeomanry were formed into fourteen brigades and the brigades were allotted to divisions so that in an emergency it would be possible to mobilise any force from a single regiment to several divisions without further reorganisation. In fact many of the mounted yeomanry formations moved according to this general plan at the outbreak of war in 1914. The entire structure of mounted Yeomanry and volunteer infantry units now came under the title of the 'Territorial Force' or popularly the 'TF' (later Territorial Army). The 'Imperial Yeomanry' title and 'IY' badges also disappeared so that the Northamptonshire Imperial Yeomanry became simply the Northamptonshire Yeomanry. Entire established regiments, as distinguished from individual squadrons, on whom a royal title had been conferred, retained that dignity – such as the Royal Gloucestershire Hussars (RGH) Yeomanry.[5] But the Royal Kettering Yeomanry, which existed for some time independently, did not bring their royal title into the larger county formation because the regiment had not had total continuity.

A further initiative by Haldane was the formation of the Officers' Training Corps at universities and public schools. This was a response to the shortage of replacement officers experienced in the Second Boer War and also meant that new officers might have a better basic professional preparation than some of the well-intentioned amateurs of earlier days. At the same time the Territorial Decoration or TD was instituted for officers who served for twenty years, with continuity from the old regime to the new.

A unique unit of the Yeomanry was founded in 1907 – a women's formation. This was the popular FANY (First Aid Nursing Yeomanry) set up by Captain Edward Charles Baker, and its task was to provide immediate nursing between the front line and the field hospitals. It was equipped at first with horse-drawn ambulances but by the outbreak of war was gradually transferring to motor ambulances.

Looking forward five years, the 1907/08 Yeomanry reform might seem to have foundered somewhat in terms of recruiting and volunteering for overseas service targets. By September 1913 the target of 312,000 Territorial Force soldiers was still a quarter short of achievement. And, of those enlisted, only about 19,000 had volunteered for overseas service. It was not until 'when the blast of war blows in our ears' in summer and autumn 1914 that targets were achieved and surpassed.[6]

This may have been of interest to the Ian Hamiltons and Eyre Cootes of the day, but for the individual Yeomen such as Arthur Arnold, continuing to serve, camp was much the same, even if a little more strictly disciplined and with somewhat more urgent tactical training. For many youths it was still a great annual adventure with added purpose. George Dixon, now less prone to raw posteriors and no longer answering back to SSMs, remembered with glee one camp catastrophe:

> It was pouring with rain when we got there and we were issued with beds which we had to fill with straw, which got somewhat wet in the process. One night the horses stampeded, pulling up the lines out of the flooded ground, and scattered all over the countryside. We had quite a time chasing them on foot and rounding them up across the downs next morning. But it was all part of the fun. Nobody complained.

The Yeomanry found that they were now more popular with the general public than in the dubious times of civil disturbances such as the Swing Riots. The RGH had a camp at Winchcombe and were left in no doubt about their popularity, whilst some of the participants of the camp revealed the depth of Yeoman tradition and commitment:

> The town went out of its way to welcome the Yeomen by erecting a decorated archway across the main street. The Cheltenham Chronicle had a picture of Bandmaster Hatton, aged eighty, who was attending. He is shown sitting up straight as a ramrod, attending his sixtieth training with the Regiment. Also shown mounted on his horse is Farrier Quarter Master Sergeant Spreadbury attending his twenty-fifth training. He won the prize for smartest turn-out …[7]

One great event united the new formations of Yeomanry, the coronation of King George V on 22 June 1911. All fifty-six Yeomanry regiments (now including two Scottish regiments) were invited, that is to say politely ordered in, and this time there was no lack of volunteers. The regiments still wore distinctive dress uniforms and, as they massed, formed a kaleidoscopic mix of colours. The only slight detriment for the traditional cavalry men was that they now paraded with rifles and bandoliers. The Northamptonshire Yeomanry detachment paraded under Maj. A.L. Renton. For the occasion the Yeomen were formed into two battalions in alphabetical order of regiments, with the two battalions lined 'Piccadilly', one on either side. The alphabetical order formation was used for this occasion only, with the Ayrshires first and the Wiltshires at the back. The Official Order of Precedence, developed according to date of foundation and uninterrupted existence as a regiment, would have placed the Royal Wiltshires first and the Ayrshires seventh.

If one camp was an adventure greatly to be anticipated, some Yeomen might have felt delighted to be told that they would have three camps this year. But the three camps in 1914 were, for many regiments, an ominous progress towards mobilisation for a major war. The Northamptonshire Yeomanry's routine camp took place in June 1914 at Milton Park, Peterborough, and rumours of impending war abounded. Troopers sought the opinions of sergeants and sergeants eavesdropped on officers. In spite of all the gossip George Dixon 'never dreamt that in five months time we should be going over to France and be together four years at war, but we got to know each other very well during those camp years'.[8]

It is interesting to follow Trooper G.H. Dixon through those last few exciting months as a typical young lad among the Territorials, and who would join the regulars to form the 'Old Contemptibles' of 1914 in France:

> I well remember going on August Bank Holiday to watch Northamptonshire v. Leicestershire play cricket. On our way back I looked in the *Chronicle & Echo* window. In it was a notice saying that we were declaring war. When I arrived home in Maidwell my mobilisation papers were awaiting me. I was order to report to the Kettering Drill Hall [and the Northamptonshire Yeomanry]. I had a hard bed on the wooden floor but was destined to have it much harder in years to follow.

Whilst Dixon was watching cricket, Cyril Day (destined to be a sergeant and win the DCM) was hard at work, it being the busy season:

> Aug. 5th – I commenced harvesting the wheat from Foot Hill field when my elder brother Alf came over the meadow calling me to say my mobilisation papers had come through. I went back to Mill Farm where mother had prepared lunch for me before I had to report to B Sqn of The Northamptonshire Yeomanry at my depot in Peterborough that same afternoon.[9]

George Dixon and Cyril Day were simple pawns in the great scheme of things planned by Haldane and which was now moving smoothly into action. For the moment the Yeomanry regiments in their allotted brigades would conform to Haldane's original vision and would mobilise to support the regular divisions which made up the first elements of the BEF. The Northamptonshire Yeomanry was already under command of the 1st (Eastern) Mounted Brigade within the 1st Mounted Division.

It was not only Yeomen that were needed, and millions of horses were mobilised, George Dixon taking part in that process:

> Farmers and anyone who had a horse suitable (14.5 hands at least) were asked to bring them to Kettering and, after being inspected by our Veterinary Officer, Captain Parks, any chosen were commandeered; in some cases, from men with perhaps only one

Cyril Day on horseback before the 1914 outbreak of war. *(NYA)*

horse, a true friend. Our officers were very sympathetic to all who lost their horses, many of whom were members of the Pytchley. Quite a lot of our horses had hunted with the Pytchley and were a grand lot, which enabled us to keep our horses to the end of the war rather than being converted to infantry, although we did not yet realise that we would be doing an awful lot of walking.

There was competition for the horses once officers had taken their pick. Cyril Day had an opportunity to move up to the front of the queue:

Some very good horses came to us from hunting stables. I happened to be on guard over them the first night so picked one out to suit myself, to which animal I afterwards became very attached. I named it Mary after my mother and sister. We picketed the horses for the first time on Derby racecourse. Again I was on guard the first night and was worked hard trying to control the horses as they kept breaking loose, not everybody being skilled at pegging down the lines.

About this time a not quite so humble trooper in the Sussex Yeomanry, Siegfried Sassoon, was offering his thoroughbred horse, 'Cockbird', to his squadron leader in the hope that the horse, relieved of a trooper's equipment burden, would have an easier life when going to war. Yeomen would later see many majors' horses savagely mutilated by machine-gun fire. Indeed, even the steeds of brigadiers and major generals were at risk in the total trench war.[10]

Haldane's reforms had fallen short of conscription or of compelling Yeomen to signed on for overseas service. Within Dixon's own regiment in 1908, when first invited to volunteer for overseas service under the Haldane system, only 10 per cent of the regiment had responded. Now with a great continental war imminent and Britain possibly threatened by German imperialistic ambitions, the response was different:

> We went from Kettering to Derby where we got our remaining horses. We were then lined up on parade and asked if we were willing to serve overseas; being Territorials we need only have served in the Home Defence, but, with very few exceptions we willingly volunteered for overseas. Those who volunteered, the great majority, then went to Houghton Regis in Bedfordshire to commence training for our work abroad.

Dixon noted the subtle change in training as the old, possibly rather light-hearted Yeomanry style and formal exercises dating from 1794 now changed into a much more rigorous system of battle preparation for both men and horses:

> We went through a severe course of military horse riding. Although most of the Yeomen were from the farming community and riders of the Pytchley and excellent horsemen, the military style was a little different. In fact some of the men were 'born in the saddle' and had, so to speak, ridden since babyhood. Now we had to ride our horses in a circle, start at the walk, then trot, canter and gallop with the stirrups crossed *in front of the saddle*, and on command we has to jump off and mount the horse *in front*! No mean task at a fast pace . On one occasion I fell off, only to hear the SSM shout 'Who told you to dismount?' We also had cross-country schemes and map-reading.

Unfortunately none of the horses were able to write memoirs, but even in England they were beginning to suffer in a way that riding to the hunt did not inflict. On their behalf George noted that 'a number of horses contracted Strangles [infectious streptococcal catarrh or equine distemper], a very unpleasant disease. Men were detailed to look after the sick horses and told not to mix them with those in good condition. With perseverance they recovered'.

The men trained and ready for war now found that they were the 1st Northamptonshire Yeomanry (officially 1/1 NY), whilst some men had been left behind to form the 2nd (1/2) Northamptonshire Yeomanry stationed locally. This unit would send up reinforcements as the '1st Line' needed them. There would also be a 3rd (1/3) Northamptonshire Yeomanry at Chichester which would be a more general training and holding unit from which men might be posted almost anywhere. The band would accompany the 1st Line but would normally serve as stretcher bearers.

The regiment was now at full mobilisation capacity and Houghton Regis camp's normal facilities were found to be inadequate. George Dixon slept in a Salvation Army hut. The local people were very kind and troopers were frequently invited to houses for tea, especially on Sundays. But the supply of peacetime Sundays was running short. Orders came to move to Hursley Park, ominously only 9 miles from Southampton docks and occupied by the 8th Infantry Division. As though in preparation for the as yet unknown trench warfare, the weather was very wet with about 6in of mud everywhere.

It was very cold and everyone tried to get an extra blanket before they were 'packed like sardines in bell tents and, for a day or two, played nap and crown-and-anchor'.

Now the move of the reserve troops of the BEF was in full flow. The crown-and-anchor boards were packed away. For the first time since 1794 the regiment started out towards the experience of real bullets, shells, bombs, gas and other horrors which called for the blue and white plumes and silver chain-mail epaulets to be packed away with the playing cards, as Dixon and his comrades travelled into the unknown:

> We set out at night to ride the distance of nine miles to Southampton ready for embarkation.[11] The horses were loaded in the bottom of the ship with fodder and equipment for them, which was a new experience for them and us and not without mishaps. We embarked on the 5th November 1914 and crossed the Channel to Le Havre – an uneventful journey. Horses and men were then entrained for Merville, the Headquarters of the 8th Division.

One anonymous but excited Yeoman wrote:

> Forth went the soldier sportsmen
> The Pytchley pastures know,
> For they who rode to hunt the fox
> Ride out to hunt the foe.

It must have caused surprise to officers and men when they learned that they were being posted to the 8th, which was an infantry division, whereas the regiment had trained as, and expected to be fighting in, a mounted brigade. Other county Yeomanry regiments would also find themselves in unexpected places alongside unfamiliar units carrying out unforeseen roles. Already it was becoming apparent that real war did not pay due respect to previously perfected planning or even the imperious dictates of generals.

CHAPTER FIVE

COURSES NOT FIT FOR HORSES
(1914–1916)

It was to be a war of terrible suffering and deprivation beyond all previous imaginings. For soldiers with fifteen years' service their Boer War memories would gradually become those of a rather good-spirited game compared with what would happen outside Ypres and on the Somme. And for those who cherished their horses the grief would be doubled.

However, for younger Yeomen setting out across the sea to a foreign country, there was still a sense of excitement and adventure. Trooper Bertie Taylor, later to become Mayor of Wellingborough, was so excited by everything that was happening that he forgot to celebrate his twenty-first birthday on the ship. He did not remember until a week later when he received his first letters and a birthday card. The rather older Cyril Day took a more serious and somewhat laconic view of events:

> We landed in France at Harise [Havre]. Was very thankful unto our God for preserving our lives and giving us a safe passage over the sea. Had to exercise the horses next morning but am sorry to say we were told to do several other unnecessary jobs just to fill in the time.[1]

The 1st Northamptonshire Yeomanry (1NY) numbered twenty-four officers and 459 other ranks on landing, with peacetime CO Lieutenant Colonel H. Wickham continuing in command. There was a standard of outstanding horsemanship which the regiment shared with several other county regiments related to their hunting links. Major, later Lieutenant Colonel, Sir Charles Lowther was Master of the famous Pytchley Hunt and was followed to war by almost all the hunt staff such as whips, second horsemen and grooms, as well as other hunt members. Typical of the officers was Lieutenant J.C. George who in 1918, whilst the regiment was in Italy, entered and won the Italian Grand National in Rome on his horse, 'Siberian'. All the NCOs were Territorial soldiers of considerable experience and a majority of troopers were from farming stock.

Senior officers of the NY were later to assume that their continuing role as a horsed regiment was due to the quality of their horses. Be that as it may, a considerable number of their horses did come from prime hunting blood lines, as a poet had written:

> In the Pytchley country you want a good horse;
> for on a bad one you will see nothing;

on a fair one you will lose your nerve;
but on the best you will be able to enjoy yourself
as you can nowhere else in the world.[2]

Recruiting had brought into the regiment some young soldiers like Bertie Taylor; however, the average age was higher and there was a clear distinction between the 1NY of 1914 and the 1NY of 1944, the latter regiment having the majority of its tank crews aged under 22. The first ten fatal casualties of the 1914 regiment had an average age of 25.8 years, the youngest at 23, while the equivalent ten in 1944 averaged 21.9 years with the youngest 19.

Although the regiment was a fairly early arrival in terms of the huge British forces which would later assemble, the first formative actions of the war had ended when 1NY landed. After Mons, the Allied armies had retreated to the Marne and then advanced again to form what would be the approximate Western Front for four years. Whilst early infantry units had suffered catastrophically in huge numbers during the fluid campaigns, the war had now become stagnant and the British Army as a whole would endure the higher aggregates of casualties caused by static trench war.[3]

The NY men soon discovered the realities of the so-called Great War of 1914–18. A mounted regiment experienced very rare, if any, spectacular cavalry charges and underwent much undignified hard labour; most tasks, if not justified by the demands of patriotism, might have been categorised as slave labour: heaving barbed wire, digging trenches, burying the dead or acting as reserve infantrymen at a moment's notice. There would certainly be no massed cavalry manoeuvres as the regiment was attached to the 8th Division of infantry whose battalions were all regulars, the only divisional exceptions being the mounted regiment, the field ambulance and the signals detachment.

George Dixon summed it up, as routine supplanted and submerged from youthful expectations:

Lieutenant Colonel H. Wickham commanded the NY when embarking for France, 1914. *(NYA)*

1939 adaptation of Kitchener's famous 1914 recruiting poster. *(NYA)*

We were soon occupied in taking up barbed wire and anything else required in the front line. We would ride our horses to within a mile or so of the front line trenches. Then, while some were detailed to look after the horses, the others would start the walk to the trenches in the dark. We would go in snake-like formation, our round mess tins fastened to the back of the men in front to enable the line behind to follow more easily. The barbed wire would be in large circles and very awkward to carry in narrow trenches with mud a foot deep. Shells and rifle bullets were continually dropping. The Germans soon got to know our route. If exposed we had to keep dropping flat and stay silent. We also had to dig trenches for the front line men to retire to. We each man were given a task, dig about six feet long, three feet wide and four feet deep, with the dirt thrown up to form a parapet.

Len Clark noted in his diary many details of the discomfort and inconvenience of this kind of life, so different to the fairly prosperous farmhouse which was his home, and indeed to the annual camp under canvas in the lush pastures of Althorp House or Rockingham Castle:

November 25th, 1914. We took up quarters at Lestrem. The horses were stabled in many places where cover could be found. My Troop were billeted at the village school. This we shared with a number of Belgian refugees, but they were in possession of the schoolroom and we had to climb a ladder and exist in the space under the roof. With no means of securing a fire it will be easily imagined how bitterly cold it was. We still have to sleep with an arm through the sling of the rifle. We had no bread to eat today and only biscuits and bully beef for dinner. Sometimes a loaf, when we get it, has to be divided between four men.

Diarist George, now Corporal Dixon, who spent most of the war trying to believe that 'the bullet would hit the other fellow', had an early narrow escape from death when the bullet did hit the other fellow who was taking George's place on duty:

We had our first casualty on one of the expeditions up the line. A trooper, Fred Sumner, was killed, hit by a shrapnel ricochet from the German front line. I think he was the first casualty in the regiment. I was not digging that night so he asked me if he could ride my rather special horse. I said, 'Yes, providing you clean the saddle when you come back'. But I had to collect the horse and clean the saddle myself. We buried him in a small garden belonging to a farmer near where we were billeted [but later moved to Vieille-Chapelle New Military Cemetery].

Christmas 1914 was famous for the mutual peace which descended on the front lines as opposing troops came out of their trenches and, in some instances, played football or sang carols in the open. For Len Clark it was memorable mainly because of the cold:

Friday December 25th – All was quiet in the line … We had no bread issued again and dinner consisted of biscuits and bully with a small portion of Christmas pudding. During the day we were each issued with the Princess Mary's Christmas Box. During the evening I sat by the fire in the Estaminet of Monsieur Lessage-Leroy to try to thaw some of the cold out of my bones, but without even the price of a glass of beer or cup of coffee as pay was so irregular, as was the food for our meals. However, I am pleased to bear testimony to the fact that our horses were never on short rations of oats or hay.

Cyril Day had received a parcel containing a plum pudding and someone bartered locally for a 'goose fowl and we enjoyed it very much. I wrote a letter and read the *Christian Pathway* (sent by Mother) in the evening.' Cecil Knight went to see a cock fight in the morning but, perhaps troubled by his conscience, went carol singing in the evening with a group of mates and raised 125 francs. George Dixon caused a minor disaster with his limited knowledge of French:

Twelve of us pals from home decided to have a supper with the contents of parcels from home, at a place called 'Marie's Café'.
    I was given the task of taking the plum puddings to the café and giving instructions for them to be brought in hot, with hot custard. Whether it was the Belgian language, or that they were like me in their cooking abilities, we ended up with cold pudding and cold custard. The fellows were not a bit kind about it.

Serious warfare resumed immediately after the Christmas pause. Many men, like George Dixon, were still finding it difficult to adjust to the vile conditions of freezing weather and inadequate sanitary provision:

My mother knitted me a body belt and sent it out with strict instructions that I was not to cast it off or I would catch cold. I HAD to cast it off or it would have walked off, it got so lousy with the filth of the trenches. We had periodic baths, big circular baths which took several of us at a time. Blankets were fumigated regularly to keep down the filth. A favourite place for the lice was in the double seams of our breeches; we would often open the seams and run a lighted candle along them and burn the blighters. A nice evening's entertainment!

Religiously inclined Cyril Day approached the new year in a sombre mood:

Jan 1st, 1915. All the Regiment were trench digging, one of our gun team fellows who was minding the horses a way back was hit with a bullet in the knee. It was raining. I didn't feel up to the mark. The work was hard and bullets were flying about a bit. One of our Regiment was killed and several others wounded. I thought what a solemn matter it was to be brought so suddenly before the Judge of all the earth. Was thankful to get back to billets.

If the Northants lads were now disabused of any notions of charging at the gallop with guidons flapping in the breeze, other Yeomanry regiments were also finding themselves posted to places or duties not previously imagined. Some, like the Leicesters, had already been in action in France at Ypres; the East Riding Yeomanry had sailed away for Macedonia and then been diverted to Egypt; several other units were also destined for the Middle East; the Bedfordshires still formed within a cavalry brigade, the 9th, but operated mainly dismounted; the Lothian and Border Horse found themselves split up into individual squadrons acting as infantry divisional cavalry; while the Inns of Court stayed in England as an officer training unit. Some units did what might be described as a circular tour: the County of London Yeomanry served in four countries before eventually arriving in France and becoming E Battalion of the Machine Gun Corps; the Mongomeryshires rode their horses in Egypt before dismounting as part of the 25th (Montgomery Yeomanry and Welsh Horse) Battalion of the Royal Welch Fusiliers; the Lancashire Hussars served as squadrons in France before becoming the 13th (Lancashire Hussars) Battalion of the King's Liverpool Regiment; the 2nd Lothian and Borders eventually traded in their horses for cycles and found themselves in Ireland; and one squadron of the Hertfordshires, after many adventures, was posted to the 15th Indian Infantry Division in Persia.

Individuals within regiments also found themselves destined for unexpected roles. Trooper V.D. Siddons was studying for the Methodist Church ministry whilst attending pre-war parades and camps with the NY. Early in the war he was commissioned and eventually qualified as a pilot in the Royal Flying Corps. He was sent to the Hejaz at the time when Lawrence of Arabia was collaborating with the Arabs against the Turks and, when required, Siddons (later MBE, DFC) acted as Lawrence's pilot. Another NY Territorial, Trooper Acland, transferred to the Royal Engineers and thence also to the Royal Flying Corps where he rose to the rank of flight lieutenant.

Arch Whitehouse was born in England but went with his parents to live in America, and on the outbreak of war he returned and joined the NY. He became disillusioned when at one point, doing dismounted work, he and his unit had to hand over some

Horses of cavalry brigade in their lines awaiting action. *(IWM Q13452)*

of their fine horses to the 4th Punjab Horse. He decided to undertake a machine-gun course and upon hearing that air gunners were needed he immediately volunteered. Issued with flying kit still stained with the blood of the previous owner, he was taken up in a plane by a Captain Clement and ordered to shoot the machine gun at a ground target while flying. To everyone's surprise he hit it. 'Holy smoke!' bawled the Canadian Clement, 'they certainly train ruddy good gunners in that Yeomanry outfit!' Arch was shot down within five hours of his first battle take-off but survived his full tour of fifty flights.

Among the most unfortunate Yeomanry units must have been the regiments who were still mounted and brigaded as cavalry, but were drafted as infantry into the ill-starred and cruel Gallipoli campaign. This was the brainchild of a Yeoman, Oxfordshire Hussar Winston Churchill, now First Lord of the Admiralty, aiming to open up the Black Sea and force Turkey to surrender. One historian points out that this was no longer a war of primitive technology:

It was the first major amphibious operation in modern warfare using such novelties as aircraft (and an aircraft carrier), aerial reconnaissance and photography, steel landing craft, radio communications, artificial harbours and submarines. Its lessons were studied by British planners for Normandy and for the Falklands assault of 1982.[4]

In one of those bad jokes inflicted upon human beings by the gods of war, General Sir Ian Hamilton, commanding the operation, might have reflected sadly on a remark he made years earlier. After inspecting Yeomanry battalions in 1908 and reporting very

The young Winston Churchill as a
Yeomanry (Oxon) officer.

favourably, he regretted that he had not had the opportunity to command such fine
men. Now his command included a Yeomanry brigade in an operation fatally flawed in
planning and extremely costly in execution.

Another outstanding historian was sympathetic to Ian Hamilton:

> He had only four British divisions and one French division – actually inferior in
> strength to the enemy in a situation where the inherent preponderance of defensive
> over offensive power was multiplied by the natural difficulties of the terrain, the Turks
> holding the commanding heights … the stagnation of trench warfare set in. They
> could not go on and national prestige forbade them to go back.[5]

In such a situation the Yeomanry brigade went ashore in a flank landing at Suvla Bay,
the first time in which such a large Yeomanry formation entered modern battle conditions. Whilst the beaches were stormed, the heights beyond provided a further area of
difficult terrain and savage defensive positions. In a typical encounter the Queen's Own
Dorset Yeomanry using bayonets took a Turkish trench. Advancing further, 'the Dorsets
were cut down by fire from a flanking position that another Brigade had failed to take.
They withdrew to the first enemy trench, having suffered severe casualties, many of
whom lying in the fire-swept no-man's-land suffered cruelly for want of help.' A day
attack having stalled, a night attack was planned:

> Led by Colonel Troyte-Bullock, the QODY moved forward across the open plain
> under artillery fire as dark settled over the battlefield. Advancing through the burning
> bushes and scrub, stepping over dead and dying infantryman and heading up Scimitar
> Hill the Yeomanry surged on. In a 'forlorn hope', men fell, struck by tracer rounds, but

the enemy's front line was captured … Having lost virtually all the officers and sixty per cent of the soldiers the QODY were temporarily amalgamated with the remains of yet another Yeomanry regiment to make a viable unit.[6]

In impossible weather conditions the Devon Yeomanry reported their predicament:

The night of 26th/27th November was marked by a terrible storm, followed the next day by heavy snow. The trenches were flooded, destroying the parapets and making them untenable. Many men were completely submerged in water, half drowned. Blankets, waterproof sheets, kits and equipment were washed away. The Regiment soon dug an emergency cover trench on Yeoman's Knoll, in the biting wind and snow, lying out in the open at night. On 28th 'C' Sqdn of the 1st West Somerset Yeomanry arrived as reinforcements.[7]

The entire Gallipoli operation was soon called off and the Yeomanry units evacuated to Egypt, having proved the merits of Haldane's Territorial Force. Perhaps the most eloquent tribute to the Yeomanry came from a Syrian military interpreter watching an attack by the Royal Gloucestershire Hussar Yeomanry. The surgeon of HMS *Euryalus* off the beaches recorded:

Towards evening the yeomanry – dismounted – advanced in close formation to make a last desperate attempt to capture Scimitar Hill. Before they deployed the enemy high explosive and shrapnel found them and – as if on parade – they opened out in a slow and dignified manner wonderful to see. Our Syrian interpreter, deeply moved, turned to me as we watched them and said, 'I know the armies of Bulgaria, Serbia, Greece, Turkey; nearly all my life I have seen them fighting but I have never seen men of such fine physique as these, nor with such bravery under fire'.[8]

Meanwhile, back in France, the Northants lads were being briefed for the Battle of Neuve-Chapelle, which began on 10 March 1915. The trench lines of late 1914 had now been consolidated and the Allied generals had to find a way through them, as there was no way to go round them. The initial plans for this almost experimental 'push' have been commended as 'original and well thought out'. A relatively brief bombardment (thirty-five minutes) of the enemy front line was followed by a further bombardment with lengthened range, which 'dropped a curtain of fire to prevent reinforcements reaching the enemy's battered trenches'. Initial success was marred by shortage of artillery shells and by command delays, followed by a belated 'press on regardless' order once the enemy had already been able to reorganise. The 'regardless' meant high, unnecessary casualties for the fighting men. For a time the NY plugged the gap between the battered 7th and 8th divisions.

The individual Yeomen knew little of the higher machinations but much of the personal pain. They knew even less of the wider political machinations:

The British had been slower than the Germans to awaken to the scale of munition supply required for this new warfare. Deliveries fell far behind contract, owing largely

A dismounted Yeoman reading his local newspaper in a Gallipoli trench. *(Keep Museum, Dorset Yeo)*

to the handicap imposed by trade-union rules. These could only be modified after long negotiation and the shortage of shells became so obvious in the spring of 1915 as to lead to a public outcry. Apart from labour difficulties the immediate fault lay largely with military shortsightedness, which manifested itself in a constant tendency to underestimate needs and underrate novelties.[9]

Much has been written about casualties, both physical and psychological. Not so much is said about the emotional impact on the individual surviving soldiers who might have been hardened to mud, anonymous body parts, rats and lice, but were in no way hardened to the loss of fighting partners with whom they had shared the most intimate of lives. Cyril Day's diary entry of 12 March 1944 illustrates this point:

> Went to the funeral of an officer and a trooper. This was the first Officer of our Regiment to be killed. He was much respected by all who knew him. Was shot in the head while in the trenches. Again I was overcome by the solemnity of death. We had about 30 casualties during the battle. We were all very sorry to lose one of our own troop, Frank Doggett who was killed by a shell at RHQ. He was a favourite with all the troop.[10]

There were many tiny tragedies occurring within the overwhelming statistical disaster of total losses. Once again Cyril Day was the observer:

> Went out filling sand bags with bricks and rubbish to finish the big redoubt a few hundred yards behind our lines. We were shelled very soon after getting at work

and had to get into the redoubt for shelter. One of our fellows named Pentlow of Huntingdon was killed by shrapnel. His younger brother, who was also in our troop, was the first to go to him and find him dead. Naturally it was a ghastly shock for the younger Pentlow who needed our arms around him. How these things bring us to see that our life is uncertain and that death is sure.

Even in the midst of death, soldiers were bothered by mundane discomfort, as Cyril confessed at that time: 'Had a boil come on my arm, had to go to the doctor to have it dressed and was put off duty for the day.' And later: 'We had a foot inspection. My feet were badly affected through being so long in the mud without having a chance to take my boots off and was told to stay behind to attend to the horses.' Foot problems were endemic and George Dixon's troop were ordered by Lieutenant Wartnaby to 'grease our feet and wear two pairs of socks to try and prevent frost-bite, a cause of many casualties at that time'. Accidents were frequent, especially with loaded rifles: in the mud Trooper Peter White pulled his rifle cover off; the rifle fired as the cover caught in the trigger, the bullet going through Peter's hand. The large numbers of horses also led to incidents; for example when a shell fell near Tom Harper's team of wagon horses and the large draught horses bolted, knocking over and injuring Tommy and his mate. Corporal Cecil Knight referred to another fearsome and frustrating hazard: 'three more killed, R. Barnwell, H. Garratt and Wilson and several wounded by our own shrapnel dropping short. Had to shift out of our own trench because of that shelling.'[11]

Writing with the benefit of hindsight, George Dixon tells graphically of an alarm and also of the long years of suffering which could await the soldier responding to such an alarm:

One night my pal and I were asleep in a Belgian wagon. We had just got fitted in when the alarm went, and we had to turn out and dress outside the wagon. It appeared the Germans had broken through near Ypres and used gas for the first time. The first patrol went out under Lt Collier (later Mayor of Northampton). Two were wounded and taken prisoner and Lt Collier's horse was shot from under him. One of the prisoners was Sgt Barrett who died later in Germany. The other was Trooper Wilford of Clipston, who was badly wounded in the thigh and spent three years in a prison camp and about one year [under a Red Cross scheme] in Switzerland. He finally returned to England and for many years visited various hospitals. This was due to the lack of care taken in the first place and, even today, after 57 years, he still has to dress the wound daily. He says it might have been better to have had it amputated at the beginning, but nevertheless he is very cheerful.[12]

Dixon also deals with a subject known to soldiers, but viewed with some cynicism by those who 'were not there' – that is to say, premonition of death:

A few days before the battle we had a supper, with parcels from home and poultry prepared by the farmer's wife where we were billeted. Lt Wartnaby gave us a talk on the forthcoming battle and told us that on no account were we to expose ourselves above the parapet out of curiosity, we should be doing no good and might possibly stop a bullet. It was ironic that he should have given us this warning when it was he who was killed in that way. He appeared to have a premonition, for one of my pals told me he well remembered him saying after the supper 'Well, good night men. If we don't meet again on this earth, we will meet in the hereafter'. [13]

The circumstances of their troop leader's death, although typical of the situation, came as a great shock to his men, as George Dixon attested. They had all gone to camp together, sailed for France together, and there worked, eaten, slept, suffered the rats and lice together with little distinction of rank:

They had been looking through field glasses at the Germans who were rushing through gaps in the trenches made by our artillery. A sniper with telescopic sights fired and killed Lt Wartnaby instantly and also put a shot through the cap of the sergeant who was next to him. I was in the next traverse when I saw the woollen beret worn by the Lieutenant fly across the back of the trench. I knew he must have been killed, We lost not so much an officer as a great friend, a real British gentleman. It was a loss we felt for some time, not only ourselves but the whole regiment. We buried him next to a trooper killed at the same time, with the usual R.I.P. cross. The next day we were given another officer but he, too, was killed, and by our own shells.

Cyril Day, skilled rider and lover of horses, also had moments of sadness of a different character, but equally disturbing:

June 9th: Sixteen of us went burying horses between our trenches off the Zonnebie road. The church at Vlamestinge was set on fire by shells and this lighted the countryside. The body of the church had just fallen in and the tower was a mass of fire when we came by. June 12th: Were up digging again at night. Had to bury a lot of artillery horses close to a village East of Ypres. These must have been dead for over a fortnight. It had not been safe to bury them before on account of the enemy shelling. The poor brutes had their harnesses on and were tied up. They must have all been killed whilst standing meekly in their lines. A very sad sight indeed.
Aug 1st: I fetched green clover from the fields for the horses, and was pleased to notice that most of the peasants round there were keeping the Sabbath.

In spite of all the horrors and tribulations the typical British Tommy remains cheerful and makes do with minor pleasures, especially the ability to scrounge a good meal. Among the lesser duties that Cyril Day's troop undertook when mounted were police patrols around Ypres to check for deserters and also to direct returning soldiers safely to their units across the featureless countryside outside the city:

We went up to Ypres on Police duty. John Scrambler had prepared an extra good dinner of stewed meat, new potatoes dug from ruined gardens round the town, boiled rice found among the ruins of a French hospital and stewed pears which were gathered from an old orchard nearby. In the evening we were back in the trenches close to Hooge and collecting equipment that had been left after the battle where the

Germans had been using burning liquid. We came into contact with gas shells still remaining unexploded but damaged and leaking. It turned several of our fellows over, fainting before we could get our gas helmets on, it made us all quite queer, but soon got over it and continued on our way.

As distinct from the normal infantryman, who manned his trench, then went back into reserve, then came back to resume trench duty, the NY varied between pioneer work, such as digging trenches and erecting barbed wire, mounted patrols of one kind or another, and also normal infantry manning of trenches. This latter stint occurred temporarily where casualties had reduced the infantry battalion to a state where it could not maintain its appointed length of trench duties until permanent reinforcements came up the line. There was no cinematographic glamour in such moments for George Dixon:

When we first had to occupy a front line trench in a normal infantry role, we walked up a communication trench, in places up to the top pocket of my tunic in water and mud. My first night was spent in a dug-out about six foot square and a foot of water. Next morning spent looking over the parapet with the aid of a periscope into No Man's Land. In between our lines and the Germans' there were several unburied bodies. At that point we were only about eighty yards from the Germans. The sun must have glistened on my periscope for it came clattering down, shot by a sniper. At night expeditions were made across No Man's Land and listening posts formed to try to get information. At one point there was a derelict house which was visited by both sides. Sometimes in the morning you would hear the Germans shout: 'How is so-and-so in England?' and they would sing English songs.

When not in the front line itself the boredom could be excruciating and the monotony is caught again and again in Cecil Knight's diary, which he must have thought rather futile as he made his entries:

June 6th: Filling sandbags at Chateaux
June 7th: Trench digging at night
June 8th: ditto
June 9th: Trench digging. Taylor wounded
June 10th: Trench digging. Orderly at night
July 4th: Trench digging for signal wires
July 5th: Trench digging at Hazerbroig
July 6th: Trench digging. Night stable guard with horses
July 7th: Trench digging at Vlomersdel
July 8th: ditto

Over a period of four months Cecil's diary ran on in the same way. His only digressions were comrades wounded, exceptional weather, fetching up stores on a wagon, or guard and orderly duties. As the regiment included a large number of farm men from the fen country who were used to working in flooded areas, the regiment obtained a not too desirable reputation for dealing with trench drainage problems.

The year 1915 passed by in France with inconclusive battles, and even when the Germans used gas there was no decisive breakthrough. There was still no way round the trench lines, and the lines themselves were ever deeper and of greater extent and engineering ingenuity. The generals would have to do something different in 1916. In Britain, work was proceeding on a secret weapon, the tank, which would eventually replace the horse in battle. But, for the time being, the only method the generals could envisage was to pour in more artillery, explode larger mines and mobilise extra infantry divisions, all concentrated on a relatively narrow area. This, they thought, might produce a gap through which the cavalry could, at long last, gallop gloriously.

The area chosen for what was popularly known as 'The Big Push' would be the plains alongside the River Somme. Suddenly the Northants Yeomen were released from the monotonous routines described in Cecil Knight's diary and were performing unexpected functions. A considerable number of men found themselves working alongside New Zealander miners, excavating and tunnelling to place mines under enemy trenches, an exploit not envisaged for the Yeomanry either by Haldane or the Earls Spencer. George Dixon responded to a call for volunteers with a knowledge of carpentry and spent months sawing, planing, hammering, preparing huts, bridges, trench duckboards and ladders ready for the Somme offensive, in a team with Highlanders and Durham Light Infantry mates. At that point Lieutenant Colonel A.G. Seymour took over command from Lieutenant Colonel Wickham who had earned a CMG at Neuve-Chapelle.

George Dixon was then sent on a mission, which caused him much surprise and some pangs of conscience whilst great battles were raging. He was told to take two men and six horses to a Royal Flying Corps airfield. He discovered that the horses were to be used for polo, which the pilots played across the airfield when not on duty. 'They would send me a type-written note each morning to tell me what horses they would want.' Some of the pilots had their own horses but others were novices at polo. George's first problem was that the RFC quartermaster system could indent for petrol and oil but not for oats and hay. The RFC also allowed a rum ration every night, a privilege unknown in the Yeomanry. The horses sent under George's care were officers' hunters and were not accustomed to the more violent antics of the airmen:

> While there I had a horse taken ill. The pilots in their RE8s would swoop over the horses' lines and scare them. They also were rough in their polo games. This horse was covered in white lather. A chill, I thought. Unfortunately it was Major Nicholls' favourite polo mount. I gave it a medicine ball. I had not given one before. The correct way was: hand in the horse's mouth and drop it down the throat. I could not manage that, so I stuck the ball on the end of a stick and pushed it down the throat. The horse did not seem to improve. I had to send it to the Veterinary Corps who fortunately saved it for Major Nicholls – and saved me from the major's wrath.

When all the huts, bridges and ladders were ready, and the armies assembled, the Somme battle began on what is regarded as the worst day in the history of the British Army: the British lost 57,470 casualties, 19,240 killed. The overall battle continued in the form of twelve separate battles over the period to 18 November, and it has been observed that 'battalions from every infantry regiment in the British Army at some staged were stationed there, thus the Somme has a unique place in British social and military history'.[14] However, the failure to make a significant breakthrough meant that there was little opportunity for exploitation by cavalry and so hundreds, if not thousands of cavalry horses were spared from slaughter at that point of the war, although horses with other functions continued to suffer.

Of future interest to the Yeomanry regiments, indeed to all cavalry regiments, were the events of 15 September 1916 when, during the Somme battles, the first tanks appeared. Liddell Hart commented:

> Their early employment before large numbers were ready was a mistake; losing the chance of a great strategic surprise, and owing also to tactical mishandling, and minor technical defects, they had only limited success. Although the higher military authorities lost faith in them, and some urged their abandonment, more discerning eyes realised that here was a key which, when properly used, might unlock the trench barrier.[15]

It is unlikely that, when the news of the amazing invention became generally available, many Yeomanry officers foresaw that this new ugly, noisy, smelly, trundling leviathan would eventually replace their sleek and speedy thoroughbred horses. Or that the elite hunts like the Pytchley, the Quorn or the Beaufort might no longer be the main providers of ready-skilled and enthusiastic personnel.

During the long period of the Somme battles, several county Yeomanry regiments, like the NY, were split into squadrons to undertake the most urgent front-line support tasks needed. Several regiments were being amalgamated as infantry battalions to replace the massive number of infantry casualties. Other regiments were facing the Turkish Army in Egypt, still with hopes of finding an opportunity to go into action in their preferred mounted role.

To paraphrase an old saying, 'All war and no play makes Tommy a dull boy'; it was well understood that in between the horrors of battle Tommy Atkins needed recreation and this was available in many forms, such as the polo played by RFC pilots using NY ponies. Among the front-line infantrymen there was often a football in evidence. One extreme form of sport was enjoyed by the Royal Gloucester Hussars (RGH) Yeomanry over thoroughly unsuitable and challenging Egyptian desert terrain. The RGH supplemented their pack of hounds with new recruits from the Cairo Lost Dogs Home. In the words of the Yeomen: 'Lost dog though it may be, from the moment of purchase it is honoured with the name of Hound.' On one occasion with a field of about a hundred the 'Yeomanry Hounds' raised a jackal and pursued it through orange groves and over the sands. The riders galloped dangerously across a wadi (dried river bed) and over trenches but were held up for a while by old barbed-wire entanglements. They were inspired forward by shouts of 'Halloa forrard' from a doughty corporal 'in charge of some natives', but the jackal disappeared among houses. Certainly a course not fit for quality hunt horses. However, such gallivanting was only a brief intermission in the dread realities of continuing war, with no quick end in sight in the East or West.

As 1916 rolled on towards 1917 and the intensity of battle decreased, the Yeomanry returned to the mundane monotonous routines illustrated by Cecil Knight's diary. That other diarist, Cyril Day, now a sergeant, noted a normal day's duties:

November 2nd – 4am I was on patrol along the front trench. 7am breakfast. 7.20 went back about a mile with party to fetch water from Brigade HQ. 10am to 12 trench patrol. 1pm dinner. 2pm wrote a letter and inspected trench mortar and machine-gun positions. 4pm tea. 5 to 6pm stand to. 6 to 8pm trench patrol, had a nap until 11pm and then went out with an Officer and a Corporal on a listening patrol between the lines. After crawling around for some time we finished our job which was to find out whether the enemy had occupied an old house in No Man's Land.

As enemy soldiers were heard talking in the house and the mission orders did not include attacking them, the officer ordered a return to the trenches, each one to find his own way crawling around the many shell holes, and their progress interrupted by bright flares fired from time to time. Day, a very religious man, attributed his return to the fact that 'the Lord was with me as I am not too good at remembering the way'. Apparently the Lord was not with the officer and corporal because they were never seen again and were posted as 'missing'.

During the war a firm spirit of camaraderie had developed between most officers and their men. Often a blind eye was turned and allowances made for the mental impact of war on the men. An NY party under Lieutenant Benyon had been burying unknown bodies who had been lying in no-man's-land for some time, the most loathsome of all tasks, apart perhaps from burying their horses. As they made their way back to billets Trooper Barnes noticed that Trooper Tucker was not carrying his rifle. He mentioned it to Lieutenant Benyon, who replied, 'Carry on. Ignore it!' The loss of a rifle was, of course, a very serious offence. Back in billets the men were settling down when Lieutenant Benyon entered carrying a rifle, which was not the one left behind by Tucker. Benyon's only comment was 'Get the number off that rifle. Don't ask questions and be more careful next time.'

Yeomen also had frequent reasons to be thankful for their officers' ability to read ground, acquired in the first place by hunting the fox. George Dixon sang the praises of such men:

> Gommecourt was in ruins. It had been taken and retaken several times and it was said there were sixteen lines of trenches with barbed wire in between. Patrolling in the dark in the area was fraught with problems of navigation. Sometimes on those excursions we would be led by Capt Litchfield, who was later the Secretary of the Pytchley Hunt. It was quite uncanny; he would lead us across country noticing all the signs such as shattered trees, pools of water, ruined churches and so on, taking us to points in the barbed wire entanglements where we could pass through, never once failing in his objective.

In view of the hunting cross-country skills of Captain Litchfield, there was a minor sensation in the NY ranks when a new officer arrived, a sensation both in respect of the identity of the officer and also of his abilities, or lack of. This was a Second Lieutenant Leslie Howard, born Leslie Howard Steiner, a surname which his Jewish family changed at the beginning of the war to the less Germanic-sounding Stainer. Howard was already a known film actor having taken part in the 1914 propaganda film *The Heroine of Mons*.

Later he would become world famous for starring in *Gone With The Wind*, *The Scarlet Pimpernel* and in 1942 *The First of the Few*.

However, what distinguished him in the Yeomanry was that he had never ridden a horse and had to be taught to ride. Before the war there had been a minority of newly joined troopers who were not of farming stock and who had needed to be taught to ride. But this was the first NY officer who, after commissioning, had to be taught to sit on a horse.

Perhaps the arrival of this reinforcement officer was symbolic of what was now happening in many British Army units of all types: a dilution of the overall skills of a unit, compared to its level of skills at the war's commencement, due to the huge and continuing roll of casualties and the frantic need for any available hurried replacements to fill the gaps.

Leslie Howard's military career was abruptly cut short by shellshock. This was also a significant time because old attitudes towards 'nervous breakdown' were changing. On 16 March 1915 pioneering psychologist Dr Charles Myers had taken up a post at Boulogne base hospital to deal with shellshock cases and within a year saw over 2,000 patients. However, shellshock was still classified under two headings: 'W', the direct effect of wounding, and 'S' or sickness, not the immediate impact effect. At least for Howard and other sufferers of the condition, psychiatric treatment was evolving.

CHAPTER SIX

THE SLAUGHTER OF THE HORSES
(1917–1918)

At the very time when the Northants Yeomanry lads and their horses, and those of other county regiments, were about to enter upon their most traumatic and gory experience of the war, meddling bureaucracy reared its unwanted head. War Office reforms, not as relevant as Haldane's, ordained that all Yeomen should be renumbered. If there was an irrelevance amid the slaughter, filth and confusion of the Western Front, this was it.

As a unit of the Corps of Dragoons, the NY men were now allocated the numbers 145,001 to 150,000, effective 3 April 1917. From the Haldane reforms of 1908 onwards Territorial Force units had allocated their own three- or four-digit numbers in sequence to their recruits. So NY's Ernie Stubbs had always reported himself on parade as '1528 Private Stubbs, E., sir!' Now all TF soldiers had to learn their new numbers according to their corps and Ernie now became 145677, fortunately a fairly easy number to learn. The nomenclature was further complicated because Ernie was known within his regiment as Trooper Stubbs, but even on his medal index card he was listed as a private.[1]

Unexpectedly, a 2NY squadron from the home base was alerted to move to France. It arrived behind the front line as a mounted squadron not knowing what fate awaited it and for a while did little. Then, to the men's great surprise, and no little displeasure, their beloved horses were taken away; they were introduced to the new tanks, which none of them had ever seen before, and were absorbed into the infant Tank Corps. So at least one squadron of Yeomanry were already moving from the splendour of the horse manoeuvres to the mundane slog of the armoured regime, which would be the role of many Yeomen in the years to come.

These were momentary diversions before 1NY, with others such as the Essex Yeomanry and the 10th Hussars, were offered a fleeting vision of a traditional cavalry charge during the Battle of Arras. However, this soon faded into the reality of probably the most appalling losses to cavalry men and horses since the Charge of the Light Brigade. It all started rather quietly for George Dixon:

> I remember riding up the cobble-stoned main road lined with trees shattered and camouflaged with sacking to prevent anything being seen by the observation balloons of the Germans. There was a lot of traffic moving up for the battle: Infantry, Cavalry, Artillery,

Ambulances, etc. We passed a railway station, very much in ruins, where we joined other cavalry units. We rode to a place called the Triangle, a sort of junction of the railway of that shape. The embankment had been undermined by the Germans and made into large dug-outs capable in total of holding hundreds of men – so we had good beds for the night. The weather was awful for April, with snow and hail, the snow lying six inches deep, and we were sorry to move away from our borrowed dug-outs.[2]

Sergeant Cyril Day was involved in one of the initial probes on 9 April 1917 and had prayed before moving, 'Cover my head O Lord in the day of battle'. He then asked himself, 'Why should I be singled out for such special care?' There was no time to await divine answers although such Biblical emanations as burning bushes and quaking earth were much in evidence:

We reached the outskirts of Fampoux and were fired at from our right. I had to take four horsemen and horses, dismounted due to conditions underfoot, over a very steep treacherous hill to drive out the enemy who were firing at us. We found about four or five Germans holding a house near a level crossing over the railway. It also crossed the river Scarpe. We immediately opened fire, killing three and took two prisoners. Another German ran to the right and as we fired he seemed to have slipped. But he returned fire bringing down one of our horses. We managed to hit him. Also here were two 8 inch German howitzer guns. Others of our troop took them out, killing one German and taking another prisoner. The rest fled.[3]

Other Yeomen were not so concerned about possible divine protection and tended to approach danger in a more phlegmatic way, as did Corporal Cecil Knight in his brief diary notes: 'Stayed out all night. Standing to, side of Railway embankment. Heavy shelling. Lt Chaplain killed. Then advanced guard. Lt. Bruce wounded. Lost several horses. Rough time.'

Cyril Day, putting aside heavenly doubts and facing earthly realities, now found himself continuing the action which earned him the DCM:

The night was very cold, it started snowing in the early morning. The enemy were still holding a bridge about 500 yards further on. I took a patrol and crept along the side of the railway. No one was on the bridge but while we were there one of their machine-guns opened fire only a few yards in front of us. We had to keep low and crawl back 500 yards to our horses but returned safely. The infantry came up and got in touch with us about 3am. This was a relief to us as this was an unprotected flank held by our troop and the ground was very favourable for the enemy to attack us. The Cyclists took over our position about 6am.

The Official History has pointed out the wastefulness of having three cavalry divisions waiting for years in France with no real possibility of a massed mounted attack across multiple trenches guarded by barbed wire and machine guns. However, 'one small cavalry unit did prove its value on 9 April, the 1/1 Northamptonshire Yeomanry … joining the Cyclist battalion … This oddball assortment of cyclists and horsemen … was to secure all road and railway bridges across the river [Scarpe]'. The cyclists were 'forced to dismount and carry their cumbersome machines over shell holes and marshy ground'. Once that obstacle had been overcome horsemen and cyclists charged at speed through the gap in the German lines and by 9 p.m. had achieved all their objectives, riding through Fampoux and bivouacking in the Feuchy marshes.

Among the Yeomen was Sergeant Bertie Taylor of B Squadron, the 1903 boy rubbish collector at a penny a day, who felt a sense of release after waiting over two years for a free gallop at the enemy:

> The shells were dropping fast and thick, then we came to some slit trenches and we just jumped these with the horses squealing – just like a hunt! Then we passed through our leading troops and I remember seeing a lot of Scottish soldiers just lying there machine gunned. Hell of a do they had. Soon we got into Fampoux and the first thing we did was water our horses in the Scarpe. After we had mounted up again we came under shellfire and one of our officers, Captain Jack Lowther – who had an enormous nose – had the end sliced off by a piece of shrapnel. Well, we laughed didn't we as he coolly got off his horse, picked up the end of his nose and wrapped it in his handkerchief.[4]

The stress of war often engendered an almost hysterical response to anything remotely humorous, as with Bertie and his mates laughing at Jack Lowther's considered coolness. (Jack, later Colonel J.G. Lowther OBE, DSO, MC.) In moments before the same action, George Dixon had suffered a moment falling somewhere between embarrassment and comedy. Captain Litchfield chose to ride George's much-envied usual mount and George was left with the captain's huge horse measuring 17 hands high:

> I would have been better off if I could have carried a ladder to mount. The girths of the saddle were difficult to get tight with frozen fingers. I would get about half way up, then the saddle would slip and so I had to start again. The C.O. Col Seymour called for the captain. The captain jumped off his horse and left me to catch it. I did this smartly, as I thought, but I got my greatcoat caught in my sword hilt and the reins mixed up and began going round and round in front of the C.O, who was standing at the mouth of his dug-out. However, not a word was said. But I felt like a fool. We continued to advance by the Scarpe river. We went so fast and bypassed the Germans. The Adjutant was wounded, Capt J.G. Lowther, and was replaced by Capt Litchfield. We had overrun several pockets of Germans but these soon ferreted out. The weather was still very bad and we stayed out all the night with the horses ready saddled up.

Another account, relying mainly on Bertie Taylor, said that 'they galloped through Arras, outstripping the others [cyclists and infantry] to such an extent that the following day they were so far ahead that they could see the Bosch [sic] reserves massing for miles'. They saw Arras in ruins, the 'great cathedral lying in great heaps of masonry choking the narrow streets up to it. The fine houses round the square looked as though some Titanic gale had torn down the fronts … saw pianos open with music on the rest, dining tables still containing unfinished meals, bed clothing and contents of wardrobes flung pell-mell about the rooms, curtains flapping in the breeze like rags on a corpse.'

There was a brief delay whilst generals consulted and eventually ordered the massed cavalry to move up ready for a further advance towards Monchy-le-Preux. Unfortunately the delay would give the Germans, always swift to react, just time enough to reorganise and would prove fatal to the cavalry. Brigadier General Bulkeley-Johnson was the commander within sight and hearing of the continuing infantry action and had to take the final decision as to where and when to let loose his 8th Cavalry Brigade. He ordered the Essex Yeomanry and 10th Hussars to circle around Monchy, but if they encountered heavy machine-gun fire they should swing into the relative shelter of the village and support the infantry.

All the cavalry out in the open with their horses were enduring a night of Arctic weather. Bertie Taylor recorded:

> The snow and the bitterly cold weather were almost as hard to endure as the shells. What a night! No cover save the sky and snowing like the deuce. We kept the saddles on all night and in the morning you could hardly distinguish the saddles from the horses so thick was the snow. At daybreak we dug our equipment out of the snow and prepared to go back, thinking the weather made cavalry work impossible. Not one of us could hold a limb still – we were so cold and famished.

George Dixon was relieved, after the night static in the open, to be ordered to mount and move forward at the trot to a spot near Monchy, unaware that they were destined to have their heaviest casualties of the war; indeed the highest casualties the regiment would suffer on a single day in two world wars:

> We arrived at the base of a hill. Other cavalry regiments were on our right and left and they were ordered to charge and the Germans gave them all they had. It was soon a massacre – horses and men blown up, some riders trailing dragged by the stirrup. We had a good view from the base of the hill and then it was our turn. We too were ordered to charge. We passed some infantry who cheered us – we were the first cavalry they had ever seen in action. My horse just flew over the shell holes. Shells and bullets were falling all around us.

Cyril Day, also astride a galloping horse and in imminent danger of death or wounding, could not ignore the incredible panorama around him, so different to anything he had ever seen before:

> We went up at a gallop, the enemy simply pouring shells at us. It was a wonderful sight, the ground was covered with snow, the air keen and frosty and the sun shining, making the frozen breath of hundreds of horses look like white smoke pouring from log fires. 'A' Squadron dismounted in the village for action. Field guns and machine-guns were sweeping the country and cutting horses and men down everywhere. It was like being shot in a trap and everyone wanted to go on but finding it absolutely impossible to get through the blocked streets.

Bertie Taylor had observed that the Essex Yeomanry were charging ahead and then heard the command for his own NY squadron to follow on their flank:

We got over the top of the rise and there it stood, red bricks showing – Monchy! The snow was laying thick, the wind freezing and at this point some of our horses collapsed, buckling the swords of their riders. We extended into one long line, a bugle sounded and we charged! Over open ground, jumping trenches, men swearing, horses squealing – a proper old commotion. We had come under heavy fire and some of the saddles had been emptied. But the horses knew what to do better than we did and galloping past me came these riderless horses. Mine, poor devil, had been wounded badly in the coronet [ankle area] so I pulled him up and dismounted and had a look at him. Well he looked at me and there really were tears in his eyes. Poor devils, they know, you know. Another one came flying past me with half his guts hanging out. Well, my horse perked up and we rode on after the others. I caught up with Mr Humphries when a shell exploded beneath his horse, and split him like a side of beef hanging up in a butcher's shop. Both horse and rider were killed instantly.

Perhaps, by this stage of the war, the ordinary Yeomen in dire danger were quite aware that rank granted no privilege in such a battle, and Brigadier General Bulkeley-Johnson himself had paid the ultimate price. Watching the advance on foot, he had been advised to get down low and crawl from shell hole to shell hole. He felt it was undignified and a bad example, so insisted on walking upright. A sniper's bullet smashed through his cheek and penetrated the brain. This meant the command devolved on Lieutenant Colonel Whitmore of the Essex Yeomanry, who was in the devastated village and who had to try to co-ordinate the widely spread and rapidly moving cavalry. Another person in the charge, Trooper Jim Ashton, shared Bertie Taylor's experience:

We lined across a huge field and charged into a terrific bombardment. As we galloped down the hill men and horses were blown up by explosives and we passed hundreds of dead and dying. The shell holes everywhere made matters worse. When we entered the village what a sight met our eyes! All the way up the main street were dead men and horses, fellows groaning, horses whinnying and kicking; one licking his dead master's face; and infantry lying on every side. I came a cropper over a shell-hole and, as I was remounting, noticed in the next hole a Lewis gun team of six men and the machine-gun. I shouted 'Cheerio, boys!' but no answer came – they were all dead.

As the village was impassable to mounted men squadron buglers sounded the 'Retire!' Bertie Taylor marvelled to see that the riderless horses, which had reached the village first, were also the first to lead the retirement without any human intervention except the bugle notes. As the withdrawal reached the bottom of the hill it became apparent that Lieutenant Colonel Seymour was missing. Volunteers were called for and two selected to go back to the village amid the continuing enemy artillery bombardment. The colonel was found wounded and his rescuers were later decorated for their bravery. Lieutenant Colonel Sir Charles Lowther, huntsman supreme and Master of the Pytchley, then took command of the regiment.

If the Northamptonshire Yeomen had suffered much, then at least two other horse units suffered even more, to say nothing of the shattered infantry. Trooper Clarence

Garnett of the Essex Yeomanry had been among the first to ride into the village of death on his horse, 'Nimrod':

> I had not been there long when a light shell came through a gap in the cottages and cut down our officer and most of the others. Nimrod was terrified and he reared up violently, dragging me along the street for some yards until I was forced to let go. I never saw him again after that. I wandered along the street and into the main square which was simply covered with dead men and horses. To my horror I saw one of our own blokes cut in two at the waist. One half of him was on one side of the street, the other on the other side. Later that morning it started to rain and I swear the streets of Monchy ran red with blood, human and equine mingled together.[5]

Garnett was by no means exaggerating. Second Lieutenant Alan Thomas said, 'the sight that greeted me was so horrible that I almost lost my head ... as far as one could see, lay the mutilated bodies of our men and their horses ... bodies stiffened into fantastic attitudes. All the hollows of the road were filled with blood. This was the cavalry.' Two bleak statistics underline the horrors: *All* the horses of C Squadron, 10th Hussars were killed, and in 1NY more horses were killed than the total of humans killed and wounded.

In a moment of black comedy amid the spreading tragedy, Trooper Doug Simmonds of the NY was for a while in danger of being charged with desertion in the face of the enemy, court-martialled and shot at dawn. He had been sent to spot for the artillery but as the chaos worsened in the village he began to help the wounded. Back at the regimental rendezvous the routine roll call failed to elicit a response from Trooper Simmonds, D.H., and nobody could account for him, dead or alive. On his return his story was not believed at first and he was made to detail all the wounded whom he had helped in the village, including those who had died. He remained under suspicion. However, once checks had established that Doug had indeed performed heroically he was awarded the Military Medal (MM).[6] Five other Military Medals and two Military Crosses (MC) were earned by the regiment. Doug was also Mentioned in Despatches on another occasion. What cheered Cyril Day was not the hope of an award but the sight of 'the transport wagons as we had had nothing to eat for three days except what we carried in our haversacks'.

Immediately after the battle the then Major Sir Charles Lowther, Bt, wrote home to his wife from Habarcq on 14 April 1917. He remembered at the peak of the battle meeting his colonel 'Archie' (Lieutenant Colonel A.G. Seymour) 'wandering around, not remembering anything owing to getting a brickbat on the head'. The writer thought it was a poor way to lose so many officer friends, about fifty men and eighty horses, although all the men were splendid in their steadiness. He continued:

> All the hunt servants came out all right. Only [Lance Corporal] Agutter got 2 in the back but did not report sick until the following day when the Doctor pulled the bits of shrapnel out of his back, rather a good affair on A's part considering his horse was shot from under him, too. I wish [brother] Jack had not been hit as I need him badly. There is no one who knows anything about the future due to the high casualties of experienced officers including the corps commander. I have got to write the report

on the whole proceedings. We had a most touching farewell to Archie who, although wounded, spoke awfully well to the assembled regiment before they took him back. The acting Corps Commander has recommended me for command of the Regiment!

It is doubtful which, for the average soldier, is the worst experience: killing and being killed or later burying the dead. As indicated throughout the Arras narratives, the mind oscillates between moments of great human, almost animal exhilaration and the extremes of terror which can paralyse the mind. There is neither excitement nor mental refuge from the sadness and obscenity of clearing a battlefield. Again it was George Dixon who was able to put such thoughts down on paper:

> A few nights after this I went on a burying expedition. This was a night I shall never forget. There were hundreds of bodies lying about and on our way up we found a trench full of dead bodies. They had either just received their mail or were taking it up to the front line. I picked up a letter addressed to P.A. Neale of the 4th Worcesters. We were ordered to fill in the trench, which became their grave. We collected several bodies and placed them in a circle sloping down into a large shell hole, after taking their identity discs. In the distance, in the darkness, frogs were croaking in a pond, making this a really ghostly, uncanny scene, to give it a biblical term 'An Abomination of Desolation'.

Major battle actions, such as 1NY's at Arras, were only a few days' suspension of what might be termed normal war service: continuing monotonous routine, always in some kind of danger, frequently dirty, hungry and lousy, the routine broken from time to time by homeland leave, then further training, often for situations which would never be encountered. When Cecil Knight's turn for leave came round in late July he went off to Northamptonshire for fourteen days. As the farm work at home was in full swing he reported to the depot and was awarded a further nine days of agricultural leave. His thoughts on return to the trenches from the clean, golden fields of England are not recorded. Another trooper, Alf Norman, was allowed a full month's agricultural leave extension during the peak harvest period.

It was now apparent to regimental officers, as well as to other ranks (ORs), that, in spite of the initial excitement as of the hunt, there was no glory to be found in the mad gallop against machine guns and barbed-wire entanglements, under a storm of well-directed artillery fire sending down lethal shrapnel and erupting under horses. The riders suffered the double shock and bereavement of seeing both their own mounts and their human mates massacred. Most of the men were convinced that their horses could weep as well. Until the vast wire entanglements and deep-dug redoubts were finally breached in late 1918, the cavalry would have no way through places like Monchy.

Before that, other Yeomanry regiments deployed in the Middle East would have opportunities of advancing at the gallop in open warfare, the Warwicks and Worcesters sharing perhaps the last charge against enemy guns. Other regiments were also moving through historic places of biblical interest: Jerusalem was captured and the Gloucesters took the town of Nazareth. But they too would first have to slog through similar travails of trench warfare against the Turkish Army, even if the slog led through parching sand rather than soggy mud.

Yeomen loved their horses and where possible buried them as in this horse cemetery, 1914–18. *(IWM Q25763)*

Those regiments were also having to encounter problems not known to the English country hunts or even regiments on the Western Front. One tactical fact was that the more numerous British Army guarding the Suez Canal had to stretch itself out along the entire length of the canal, whilst the Turks, with fewer troops, could quietly assemble a locally overwhelming force to strike through a small area of the vast desert. Another problem for individual soldiers was the difficulty of digging trenches for shelter in sandy ground which collapsed again and again during the digging. Yet a further constant problem was the finding, or delivering over long distances, of water in such a terrain, the Sinai desert being one of the driest places on earth. On one particular day the RGH had, apart from about 350 humans, some 456 horses, thirty-eight mules and sixty-two camels all needing regular water to drink.[7] And there were many such units spread out between the few available wells. One story concerned an Australian trooper who saved a part of his water ration, which he poured into the crown of his slouch hat. With this he managed to wash his feet. He was about to throw away the remaining slops when two other men rushed up, grabbed the hat and drank the water.

Back on the Western Front the Northants lads had no visions of anything but a continued routine of dull slaving, back and forward to the trenches. On 29 September 1917 Sergeant Cyril Day recorded 'Enemy planes were over dropping bombs most nights. On Thursday they hit the guard tent of the Cyclists, killing one and wounding six. Several bombs were dropped round the farm in which two of our troops were billeted.' Aeroplanes were now designed and equipped to bomb accurately as compared to the rudimentary 1915 plane whose pilot might lob a bomb out of the cockpit almost casually, without much hope of hitting anything vital.

An old-fashioned kind of genteel relationship existed between some higher commanders and troops. On 30 July 1917 five Yeomanry regiments were gathered well
behind the lines for further training and were inspected by the corps general (four
ranks higher than Lieutenant Colonel Lowther). He then 'sent a nice letter to thank
and praise the Northamptonshire Yeomanry for the good work we had done and said
he was sorry to see us go'. Cyril Day and his mates did not know they were 'going' but
by next day they were packed up and moving out, and the kindly general turned out
at dawn to wave them goodbye. Not quite the 'donkeys leading lions' that some critics
have deigned to call First World War generals.

George Dixon was clear in his mind that it was the quality of the regiment's horses
which led to its next assignment:

> We were sent to a refitting camp at Ayette, where we joined several other Yeomanry
> regiments. Several of the regiments were to be disbanded but owing to the quality and
> condition of our horses we were to remain as cavalry and proceed to Italy to help the
> Italians. We went to Dunkirk and trained on the beaches whilst waiting to go.

The mention of the condition of the horses is a reminder that many high-ranking
commanders like Field Marshal Haig were originally cavalry subalterns. An ex-cavalry
general, instead of peering down the barrel of a trooper's rifle or cocking a machine
gun, would be more likely to open a horse's mouth and judge its general health, later
basing his report on the efficiency of the regiment more upon the condition of the
horses rather than the cleanliness of the weapons.

A patrol of the NY crossing a river in Italy, 1918. *(NYA)*

The news that the regiment was destined for Italy was received with great rejoicing by all ranks, with a vision of exchanging the alternating soaking mud and clogging dust of France for the vine-clad hills and balmy climate of Italy. And for the horses there would be lush, green pastures and cool, crystal streams flowing down from the snow-capped mountains.

While the main British Army fought on in France and other British troops advanced with the Egyptian Expeditionary Force, great battles were taking place on the Eastern Front involving mainly Germany, Russia and the Austro-Hungarian Empire. Armies clashed from the shores of the Baltic in the north, where the Germans had defeated the Russians with a classic encircling movement at Tannenburg, to the mountainous border between Austria and Italy in the south. There, in October 1917, the Austrians had defeated the Italians in the Tolmino-Caporetto area, precipitating a disastrous Italian retreat to the River Piave, with the loss of 250,000 prisoners. Both Britain and France responded immediately by each sending out an army corps to the relief of the Italians.[8] The British corps was commanded by the Earl of Cavan.

The release from the horrors of the trenches gave the rail journey from Dunkirk to Italy a holiday atmosphere for men like Cyril Day, in spite of the slight discomforts of 'about fifth class rail coaches':

Crossed the frontier to Italy and detrained at Ventimeglia. It was a lovely morning, the inhabitants all the way down were giving us fruit and flowers. It was 10pm when we pegged our horses down ... We picketed in a field outside Rega. The Italians opened a big girls' school for us to sleep in and provided us all with mattresses ... At Allassio we put our horses in seaplane sheds on the sands ... Weather better than ever, the scenery was very beautiful. All the fellows enjoyed the ride. We had a good welcome all the way.

The Italian civilians, shocked by the apparent disintegration of their entire army, could not express their welcome warmly enough. The Northampton local newspaper reported that the troopers 'for six days rode through the Italian Riviera among masses of flowers, hailed everywhere with frantic joy by the natives'. George Dixon shared the excitement but also had a thought for some horses which were not quite so fortunate:

We were met by people strewing flowers and handing us wine and grapes. One would have thought it was a peace celebration. We travelled twenty miles each day. At one place we tied our horses up between trees with red berries and about ninety per cent of the horses were ill. It was believed this was due to the berries. About nine of the horses in our squadron died. They were placed on the beach and were skinned by the Italians. However the sharks came after them and spoiled the fishing. So the fishermen tied the horses' bodies and towed them out to sea. One of our troopers went with them. He said he never expected to get back alive. The sharks kept attacking the horses, nearly upsetting the boat, while the fishermen were cutting them clear one by one. Very nasty.

It is difficult to enter into the minds of horsemen of long ago and determine how much real emotion and sympathy they felt for their steeds. Riders in 1914–18 like those mentioned certainly experienced great empathy with their mounts. A brief glance at present-day advice for horse care shows how inconvenient it was to care for horses in battle. For example, 'a horse should never be given cold water after a hard sweaty work out'. How could this be reconciled with the NY chargers having to be watered at the Scarpe in the midst of 'a hard sweaty work out' when that was the only water available during the entire day? Or 'have water available at all times'. How could Yeomen traversing the Sinai desert have water available at all times? Or 'water and feed should be given frequently in small quantities'. As will be seen, the later stages of the NY's Italian campaign involved such rapid and lengthy pursuits that there could be no convenient frequent pauses for small meals. And the final difficulty, of course, was in considering that a horse may need 'five to fifteen gallons on an average day'. With 500 animals (2,500 to 7,500 gallons a day) in a waterless desert or amid barbed-wire entanglements on chalk downs, how impossible were the water-carrying tasks of each regimental quartermaster?[9]

Whilst the NY lads were happy to resume their role as cavalry, other regiments, particularly within the Egyptian Expeditionary Force, were suffering disappointment as they lost their horses and became infantry, equipped and denominated as such. Formed into the 74th (Yeomanry) Division of infantry, they marked their grief by taking as their divisional emblem 'the Broken Spur'. Seventeen regiments were amalgamated into eleven battalions to form the three brigades of the division. Whilst their Yeomanry designations survived partially within discreet brackets, their working titles were also infantry titles and sometimes different from the original. The Suffolk Yeomanry became easily transformed as the 15th The Suffolk Regiment; the Shropshire and Cheshire Yeomanry regiments were amalgamated and found themselves to be 10th King's Shropshire Light Infantry; the Fife and Forfar suffered a complete name change and became 14th Black Watch (Perthshire Regiment); nevertheless, the 74th performed as infantry in a manner which did not betray its enthusiastic Yeomanry traditions.

In a sense the Egyptian Expeditionary Force lost its identity as it survived massive attacks by the Turkish Army around Suez, advancing into Palestine and Syria. Some regiments like the RGH had fought hard and suffered much in the initial defensive and first abortive attacking battles. With the arrival of General Allenby and a breakthrough around Gaza, the mounted men at last had opportunities to sound the charge on their trumpets, but, to a large extent, they were ringing down the curtain on the cavalry era.

On 8 November 1917 there took place what has been described as the last classic unsupported cavalry charge (against artillery) of the British Army. In the Third Battle of Gaza the 60th Division had been pinned down by Turkish artillery fire and were unable to advance. The cavalry immediately available amounted to only one and a half squadrons of each of the Worcestershire and Warwickshire Yeomanry, a force consisting of well under 200 riders. They faced eleven artillery guns and four machine guns, and it required a full gallop over open ground with no possibility of shelter. The objective was reached, the guns were captured and the infantry were able to advance again, but at a cost: all the squadron commanders were killed; only three officers survived unscathed, twenty-six ORs were killed and 100 out of 160 horses were killed.

On 13 November, nearing Jerusalem, another Yeomanry force undertook a mixed operation involving three regiments advancing up a hill towards well-dug-in Turkish troops at the top. The Buckinghamshires, wielding swords, were able to storm their side of the hill on horseback; the leading Dorsets used rifles and bayonets as they attacked on foot over ground where horse attack was not viable; and the Berkshires carried out a normal cavalry attack, but then, on following through, reverted to dismounted advance through houses. One comment observed 'successes such as these proved the effective use of shock action by cavalry against infantry, such as had rarely been possible on the Western front'.[10]

While the Turkish Army disintegrated around Palestine, the German Army on the Western Front had been reinforced after the collapse of the Russian Army and the Bolshevik Revolution. The spring of 1918 saw the Allied armies under threat from the resurgent German forces and 'Backs to the wall!' calls were sounding ominously. Some regiments which had been fighting the Turks were hastily sent across the Mediterranean to France, while other regiments continued across Syria to Damascus and Aleppo. In the reorganisation the Gloucester Yeomen, who had previously been 'chummed' with neighbourly county regiments, found themselves brigaded with the 15th and 18th Bengal Lancers.

The NY's triumphal ride through Italy inevitably ended in the shock of renewed action, but against a new enemy, the Austrians, who came fresh from a famous victory over the Italians. Initially, serious warfare would be the order of the day, as Cyril Day's first active day revealed:

> Left regiment with two officers and a corporal to be attached 9th Devons in the front line. At 10pm about 30 of the 2nd Gordon Highlanders went out to raid the enemy's line. Owing to so many raids being made the enemy were prepared and waiting for them in much larger numbers. The Gordons were driven back with heavy casualties. The Yeomanry were to make a raid on the same place a few nights afterward. We four had to reconnoitre the ground and make the plans … we found the enemy patrols out but got within a few yards of the enemy post. They evidently saw us as we heard them shouting something like 'Enlisa' meaning no doubt 'English'.

Another man, Trooper William 'Chas' Cotton, was awarded the Military Medal for his actions in a similar miniscule but dangerous sally:

> We got Jerry [soldiers' name for Austrians as well as Germans] over the river alright. Then he made a stand outside a village. The order came to our Troop for four men to go out on a special patrol and I was chosen leader. The Colonel said there were men and machine-guns 400 yards out and he wanted them located. Away we went and I can tell you we had a pretty warm time. We found the guns and THEY found US too! I had a bullet through my rifle sling and my pal had one in his haversack! However, riding fast no one was injured. The C.O. told me he was pleased with my leading as the point man.[11]

As if there was not already enough responsibility on the NY with its normal reconnaissance duties ahead of the infantry, the regiment now had to take care of a distinguished attachment in the person of the Prince of Wales, heir to the throne. Aged 23, he was serving on the Earl of Cavan's staff. He had always been keen to experience the real conditions and perils of the front line but, under the king's orders, was restrained as much as could be done with a quite wilful young royal. In the thronged trenches of France there were no easy opportunities to evade his guardians; the more fluid action in Italy allowed him to evade minders and join the NY or other forward units. But, for the unit to which he attached himself at a particular moment, ensuring his safety was more urgent than defeating the enemy. He was popular with the troops at the time but would find a kind of notoriety with the NY in years ahead.

Now an 'old soldier' in the eyes of new reinforcements, George Dixon was surprised in 1918 to be ordered to do more training. In France there had been little demand for reading maps to move over unknown country. Now in Italy they needed smart navigation among the fields, vineyards and hills. His group was given a distant and obscure landmark to find on horseback, and then they were to mark out defence posts. They found the objective and were sitting triumphantly at the spot. At that point Major Nicholls arrived, confirmed that they were correct and then bawled: 'What I don't want to see is four of my NCOs sitting on their horses peering at their maps like four bloody owls.' For Dixon, serious business resumed soon enough:

> We first got in touch with the enemy at Vazzola. We ran into their machine-guns. Our squadron was ordered to try to get through to the place marked on the map. We ran into a machine-gun barrage. I was second-in-command of the section. We had to gallop for dear life, our casualties being one horse. I lost my tin hat but walked back and fetched it after we dismounted. Our other squadrons had done quite well. A patrol of about six men had captured two hundred Austrians. The officer in charge got the MC. The Colonel himself, Sir Charles Lowther had to beat a quick retreat when out on reconnaissance and the Austrians hemmed him in from three sides.

Next day 'passing through the cheering front line infantry and penetrating nearly ten miles into enemy territory', Dixon's group found themselves literally 'off the map' as they had ridden beyond the edges of their maps. As they continued one squadron rode into a village to find it thronged with exhausted enemy troops sleeping or sitting with their boots off by the wayside. Meanwhile, another great Territorial survivor, Cyril Day, had temporarily come to grief. Taking over from his sick SSM, Cyril's horse slipped into a deep ditch and was in danger of drowning, dragging his rider down too. 'I had to hold his head up to prevent drowning. After he came round he repaid me by plunging and laying me out a yard further up the ditch.' He was then involved in what must have been one of the last cavalry charges of the war:

> Oct 28th: Moved off at 10pm after evening prayer. Roads were packed with traffic and it took us to 0400hrs to reach the pontoon bridge over the river. The enemy had blown up the bridge but we managed to ford the river. We galloped across into a maize field and fired from our horses, returned rifles, drew swords and galloped into the enemy position. To our surprise the whole line surrendered to about out 10 of us. We each took a batch of prisoners back to our infantry who by then had reached the ford.

Our Squadron going on forward we got in front a bit so had to wait. [In the town] we took the station and fought dismounted up the street. Bullets were hitting and flying all around but only one of our fellows was killed. He was my batman.

The 1NY and North Irish Horse were preparing to advance again when the Italians warned them that the Austrians had asked for an armistice. Confirmation trickled down from corps HQ.[12] The fighting was over, but not the duties as the King of Italy wanted to review and thank the British troops. George Dixon's squadron leader, Lord Stallbridge, 'who was not keen on spit and polish', said to the SSM: 'Just let the men polish the brass butts of their rifles, that is about all the king will see.' After parading at the trot in front of and being thanked by a king, eventual demobilisation was a total and dismal contrast. Cyril Day, jotting down diary entries to the last, noted:

Feb 4th [1919]: Arrived and detrained at Cherbourg. It poured with rain on the march to the rest camp 5 miles away. All the tents were full with water coming through into them ...
Feb 6th: The engine drivers were on strike so could not get on train. Demob camp at Purfleet – officer who had our papers had not turned up. Wet and fed up. Got to Cambridge at midnight. Brother Alf waiting with the horse and trap. Reached Mill Farm very thankful at one a.m.

George Dixon heard that many horses were sold for very high prices in Italy, but 'they did not sell all the horses. They were put into different categories and I think the best came back to England.' A Northampton newspaper reported that 'animals which averaged £36 to £40 before the war fetched from £100 to £200 after going through the campaign'. The price increase may have been partially due to the drain on equine stocks caused by the horrific mortality during the war years.

It has been estimated that during the war on all fronts 8 million horses died. In 1917 'at this stage men at the front understood that to lose a horse was worse than losing a man'. Men might be replaced but horses might not.[13] To compensate for losses from 1914 to 1917 (when America entered the war) about a thousand horses a day were transported by ship from the USA to France as replacements. Many horses in France were killed by poison gas, as although they had been provided with gas masks they tended to eat the masks. The Royal Veterinary Corps treated 725,216 horses during the war, of which 529,064 were saved. The unlucky ones were part of the total of 484,000 British horses killed in action or died due to infection or exposure.[14]

One Yeomanry formation which deserves a special mention is the First Aid Nursing Yeomanry (FANY). During the war its 'Yeowomen', working directly behind the front lines, won no less than seventeen Military Medals, gained a *Legion d'Honneur* and also twenty-seven *Croix de Guerre* awards. Not many male units could equal that record.

Future 1NY regimental sergeant major (RSM) and eventually longest-serving Territorial of his day, George Jelley was as yet a boy soldier who had increased his age in order to get to France before the war ended. He was now with a Royal Artillery unit in the army moving to occupy an area of Germany, where the population had suffered greatly in the last days of war. George, scion of the Northampton leather industry, was ordered to shoot a sick horse, skin it, keep the hide and bury the body. Next day he found that local people had dug up the horse for meat.

In Everdon near Daventry, Richard and Mary Bird would mourn their son, 2266 Trooper Eric Bird, aged 19, the youngest Northants fatality. In Newark, alone, Annie Papworth would mourn her husband, 145360 Private C. Papworth, who at 44 was the oldest of the regiment's Yeomen who would not return. Perhaps the cruellest news to be contained in the ominous yellow telegraph envelope carrying its message of doom would be that sent to Gladys Tomalin in Northampton; a telegram was delivered to her after the end of hostilities, for her husband, 146135 Private Albert Tomalin, was killed in Italy on 1 November 1918 by one of the last shots fired against 1NY in the war.

CHAPTER SEVEN

PUNCTURED PRIDE
(1919–1939)

George Jelley had wanted to join the Yeomanry in 1916, but being underage and having to falsify his birth date, he found himself posted to the Royal Artillery. He was demobilised in 1919, but in 1920 saw in a Northampton newspaper an announcement calling for recruits for the revived Yeomanry; he was first in the queue.

There was a hiatus between the 1919 demobilisation of the Yeomanry regiments, in their various roles, and the 1920 revival of the regiments, not necessarily in the same roles as during the war. The Territorial Force was officially reconstituted on 7 February 1920 but on 1 October 1920 it was renamed the Territorial Army. There were also adjustments for particular roles in accordance with new strategies emanating from the lessons of the recent war. A modern-sounding element entered into public awareness with the 'Gedes Cuts': reductions in some formations due to government economies needed to balance the national budget.

The Great War had revealed that the establishment of cavalry units in the British Army far exceeded the frequency of opportunities that there would be for cavalry action in the closely targeted artillery, barbed-wire and machine-gun era. Inevitably the regular cavalry regiments would continue to supply horsed formations for the time being. This left only a few horsed units to be found from the Territorial sector, with the senior Yeomanry regiments filling requirements. So the Royal Wiltshire (Prince of Wales' Own), the Warwickshire and others following them in precedence would retain horses. It is perhaps relevant to note again that those two regiments were founded at about the same time as the Northants, but had maintained a regimental structure throughout, whilst during the 1800s the NY had, at times, existed only at squadron level, thus losing precedence.

In the confusion of the first days of reorganisation, George Jelley, to his delight, found the new NY, commanded by Major J.G. Lowther, the war-time adjutant, to be practising cavalry drill; they were riding horses, all of them hunters, in a field behind the Drill Hall. The new enthusiasts were about to receive an unwelcome shock.

In the new type of warfare horses would be largely replaced by internal combustion machines, either light tanks riding on tracks or armoured cars riding on wheels. The Tank Corps in 1920 consisted of seven tank battalions and nine armoured car companies, numbered 1 to 9. Unhorsed Yeomanry units were now formed under the aegis of the Tank Corps and wearing the tank badge, as subsequently numbered armoured car companies. For instance the Sharpshooters (County of London) became the 23rd Armoured Car Company, the Tank Regiment; the Derbyshires paraded as the 24th, and the NY fell in as the 25th. All car companies retained their Yeomanry designation in brackets. The Tank Corps itself was elevated to the Royal Tank Corps (RTC) in 1923.

These changes had a devastating effect on the new NY. When George Jelley reported for duty he found a cadre of regular cavalrymen with Captain Coles as the permanent officer, RSM Corke and QM Hyatt. Major Lowther had, of course, reverted to a part-time Yeoman in peacetime. Only six volunteers paraded the first time with George in cavalry-style uniform, but:

> As numbers increased so we were able to make progress. A number of war officers and men rejoined and by the time 1921 came round the Yeomanry spirit was once more very much alive. Training consisted mainly of foot drill, arms drill and riding drill. Later in the year came a terrible shock. We along with five other regiments were to become mechanised. Upon hearing this, sad to relate, most of the old Yeomen left. Those of us who remained awaited the arrival of the new vehicles. In the meantime our cavalry PSIs like Capt Coles and RSM Corke were replaced by Tank Corps people. We now handed in our cavalry dress and were issued with infantry uniforms. What a come down![1]

Nobody knew what to expect as none of the surviving personnel had ever encountered an armoured car close up. Few had even heard the fateful name 'Peerless', which surely meant superb or unequalled. They might later ask 'in what respect was it unequalled?' And there would have been a very rude answer. The Peerless armoured car was an urgent 1915 adaptation of the American 3-ton Peerless truck fitted with a primitive armour-plate body with an open back. Eventually it was refined to some extent, still using the Peerless truck chassis but with an improved armoured body made by the Austin Motor Company. The body contained a driver's compartment plus two turrets, each armed with a 0.303 Hotchkiss machine gun. The car weighed about 7 tons, relied on a rear-wheel chain drive, had a top speed of less than 20mph and required a crew of four to operate.

Even though there had been an interim period when the new recruits were allowed to train as cavalry, there was still a long period when training was restricted to what might be termed 'armoured car drill without armoured cars'. More urgent calls for armoured cars were being received from Ireland and from the Indian Army, as well as the 'home' companies of the Tank Corps. So George Jelley and his comrades, from Major Lowther down, paraded faithfully at weekends. It was not the sound of a silver cavalry trumpet which eventually spurred the Yeomen to mobile activity, but an 'ugly, roaring noise' full of industrial menace, as George heard it:

> After a very long time I strolled one evening to the Drill Hall and saw the gate and part of the wall flat on the ground. A small voice said to me 'the armoureds have arrived!' Sure enough they had. These were Peerless armoured cars and were they well named? Big, ugly things weighing about ten tons, solid tyres and chain drive, top speed about fifteen miles an hour – IF you were lucky. Mostly they did not go at all.

The next thing of course was to learn to handle these monsters, so most of the time was now spent in driving and maintenance lessons. I hate to say this but we all failed our first test. We blamed these ugly brutes which would not behave like decent horses would. However, next time we all passed and were ready to take our vehicles to the first camp, whenever that should take place.

The first NY post-war camp was eventually arranged for August 1922. This is recorded tersely as 'Place – Cardington near Bedford. Distance – about twenty-two miles. Time taken to arrive – all day. Comments – nothing very exciting except for frightening a few civilians and ending up in someone's front garden, the proprietors of which were not very amused.' The drivers of the Peerless armoured cars, in spite of passing their tests, had obviously not yet mastered the obstreperous beasts. Meanwhile, the Yeomen were required to wear the cap badge of the Royal Tank Corps but continued to use the 'White Horse of Hanover' of the original NY as the 'collar dog'.

By the time of the 1923 camp George Jelley had commenced his more detailed diary with illuminating glances into the excitement and sometimes chaos of the annual camps. Place – Swingate Camp, Dover:

The advance party right from the start performed wonders. Believe it or not, they actually drove the Peerless cars from Northampton to Dover. We never expected to see them. The rest of us detrained at a station about four miles from the camp site and in those days we always marched. We drew our full complement of cars and were able to operate for the first time as a full squadron. By now I was a corporal and I had as my driver one of the men who had brought one of the cars down to camp. I thought at the time how lucky I was. Training now commenced under the command of Maj Geoffrey Elwes, squadron commander, who wore white cavalry breeches.

The NCOs and troopers did not yet realise that a camp so near the White Cliffs of Dover was likely to be more perilous than in the safe haven of Althorp Park. They now found themselves hazarding their clumsy and recalcitrant vehicles along narrow tracks with very little room for error, and with the sea lapping the cliffs hundreds of feet below. Each car was sent out to navigate individually. George asked his driver if he knew the way, to which he replied, 'Yes, Corporal'. But the driver proved to be a fearless man with ambitions to drive his car around the Brooklands or Monza racing circuits:

We were going merrily down the hills, very close to the cliff edge and I was getting worried. I shouted 'Put you brakes on'. We came to a hairpin bend, he turned his wheel for all he was worth, and we finished up with our front wheels out in the empty air, but still upright. My troop leader, a new officer, came dashing up in his car and said 'Who is in charge here? Consider yourself under arrest. When you get out of this mess, follow me.' We edged back into the track, went off round another particularly sharp bend. And there was the troop leader himself with his front wheels nicely parked in a hedge – smoke pouring out all over the place and absolute chaos. I ventured to approach the troop leader saying 'With your permission, sir, I will get you out of this'. When we got back to camp the troop leader simply said to me, 'You know, Corporal, these drivers are not safe'. Later in the morning I was sent for, to report to the orderly room. 'What the hell is wrong now?' I thought. To my utter amazement I was being promoted to sergeant.

During 1922 and 1923 the NY senior officers were confronted with a rather embarrassing and perplexing problem requiring discretion and diplomatic skills. In 1921 the annual Northamptonshire Yeomanry Challenge Cup race was run at the Pytchley Hunt point-to-point meeting at the Bringstons. It was won by an old acquaintance from Italy days, HRH the Prince of Wales, later King Edward VIII and even later Duke of Windsor. It is not recorded if the prince won on merit or if the other riders discreetly forewent any opportunity of overtaking him. Whatever the case, the prince departed carrying the cup, but when the time arrived for the 1922 race the cup, which was normally held for a year, he did not reappear. Perhaps the busy prince had forgotten. By 1923, after due doffing of caps and polite enquiry, it became apparent that the royal rider had decided unilaterally to keep the cup; indeed he had had his name inscribed on the trophy. It was a story which would have echoes many years ahead.[2]

Such aristocratic machinations had little impact on the NCOs and troopers for whom the annual camp continued to be the focus of both advanced training and personal enjoyment. For men largely employed in the monotonous routine of the boot or brewery industry it was exciting to learn that the 1924 camp would once more be at Dover. Again the most insignificant events became memorable. For George the notable incident of the camp was a moment of farce.

We had one or two newcomers. It was obvious by his face that one had been in the boxing ring. I said, 'Who are you? A boxer?' He said, 'Champion of the Manchesters

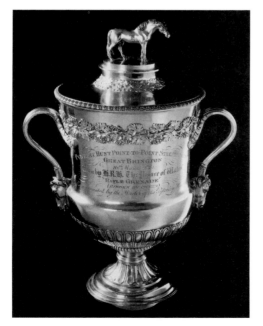

for the last three years. But everybody calls me "pet"!' In those days the catering corps did not exist. Pet was made cook. One day he decided he would give the troops a treat and make a 'spotted dog' pudding. He had the flour, he had the currants, but he had no cloth to wrap the pudding in. Being full of enterprise (as a Yeoman should) he ripped off the tail of his shirt and used that. Cor, blimey!

1921 NY point-to-point cup won by the Prince of Wales. *(NYA)*

George does not record any serious mishaps to the health of the troops as a result of Pet's ministrations. However, in 1926 higher authorities in the regiment had taken note of the continuing plight of soldiers wounded or otherwise incapacitated by the Great War. The Northamptonshire Yeomanry Old Comrades Association was founded as a charitable trust to 'establish a Fund to assist members who through age, sickness, wounds or any other difficulty are unable to maintain themselves; to obtain employment for members on discharge; to assist wives and families or widows and orphans; to maintain and promote fellowship and association between past and present members …'. The association, as extended in 1943, would outlive the active regiment.

Camps continued to provide training and holiday enjoyment for the Territorials and there appeared to be little restriction on petrol consumption. In 1925 the cars drove from Northampton to Salisbury Plain and one scheme saw them driving from Salisbury almost to the outskirts of London and back. Old soldiers like George still maintained some cavalry instincts and at the 1926 camp George was reminded by superiors that his group of soldiers was not called a 'Troop' but a 'Section'. However, officers on the armoured cars still valiantly carried whips.

Historically the Yeomanry had been recruited from smallholders, hunt servants and the like, but in urban areas respectable people such as small tradesmen had joined. Now, with increasing unemployment in the late 1920s, Sergeant Jelley noticed a new type of Territorial coming to camp. 'I had a rare old bunch of rough necks … but they make good soldiers.' They were also much harder to discipline and more prone to drunken outbursts. 'But let me say that they never let me down on parade.' In one hilarious episode, a tent full of men back from a pub crawl tied their tent shut and refused to put the lights out. When the adjutant's shouted orders failed to produce results the adjutant, a huge 20-stone man, simply leapt on top of the tent, brought it crashing down and walked away, leaving the defaulters smothered and squirming in the dark.

Another hilarious episode was not appreciated by officers of another regiment, but aptly underlined the changes in the nature of warfare. Critics have since noted the fact that the British Army, having introduced tank warfare, was slower to adapt to 'armoured doctrine' than other countries and tended to hold on to cavalry traditions. Sergeant George Jelley in all innocence recorded a significant event near Colchester camp in 1929:

> It is interesting to note that in spite of our conversion to armour, the Officers always paraded as Yeomen, booted and spurred. We had an exercise against another cavalry unit, whose name I choose not to remember. Really it was too easy. Seeing our approach, they smartly dismounted, one man holding four horses, and took up infantry positions in the hedge. We immediately turned our cars on them, smashing into the hedge. They scattered in all directions. We then aimed our cars at the horses and they all bolted. The regular colonel was not amused. Perhaps not very sporting war but very effective! This was the last camp where we held equestrian sports.

Having wrestled manfully with the ponderous Peerless cars for a decade, the Yeomen were encouraged to hear that a new armoured car was on the way with a truly peerless name, the Rolls-Royce. These armoured cars were indeed constructed on the chassis of the contemporary Silver Ghost civilian car. Weighing only 4 tons compared to the Peerless' 7 tons, they could achieve 45mph rather than the older vehicle's less than 20mph. Equipped with a machine gun in a revolving turret, the car was further strengthened by having twin rear wheels, so that a single puncture would not incapacitate the vehicle. The Rolls-Royce had been used in Dublin as early as 1921 but, after allocation to regular units, was only now becoming available to the NY in 1929 and 1930.

Although some new recruits coming into the regiment may have been of a rather different type to the original Yeomen, the officers continued to draw on eminent county families: Major G. Elwes, who notoriously wore white cavalry breeches, commanding 1925–30, and Major A.F.G. Renton 1930–40. On 8 November 1930 the annual dinner was held with the band playing *John Peel* and *Auld Lang Syne*. The usual loyal toasts were drunk to 'The King' and 'The Regiment'. Then Colonel Lowther arose and proposed 'To Foxhunting!'

In 1930 George Jelley and three other Territorials obtained special leave from work, George from the Northampton brewery, and spent a month at the Driving and Maintenance School of the RTC at Bovington. They were to become the instructors within the NY on the Rolls-Royce armoured car, only a couple of which were delivered to Northampton at first. Arriving at the annual camp, this year 'an ideal site' at Shoreham, to take delivery of these splendid new vehicles, they were surprised to find all the tyres worn out, the cars having been handed down from a regular unit. The next day, the first training day as sections, they were ordered on a 100-mile run, but all cars failed to return within the time limit because of frequent punctures. Pride in the new Rolls-Royces was well and truly punctured.

As the 1930s progressed, Hitler took power in Germany and the resurgent German Army developed the most radical ideas of tank warfare, which would be justified by the annihilation of the powerful French and British armour during the blitzkrieg of 1940. In Britain, however, 1933 was 'austerity year' and there was no annual camp for the NY, although a few days were spent at Ludgershall on Salisbury Plain by a few officers and men who went at their own expense. George Jelley was also sent on a refresher course on the Vickers 0.303 machine gun, on which he had been an instructor for some time. When the test took place at the end of the course, George went through the stoppage exercises with practised efficiency, reacting to the sudden call 'Stoppage!' from the examining officer. Then the examiner commented, 'I am not sure if I can pass you.' 'Why not, sir' asked a perplexed George. 'Because you must have anticipated the stoppage call, you were so quick.' This left George mystified: how can one anticipate a machine-gun stoppage?

The year 1934 saw the camp at Rodean and the Territorials allowed to play cricket on the girls' school ground. It also revealed once more to the ORs something of Britain's inefficiency in military provision. Again Sergeant Jelley was observing:

> The most exciting part of our training was the treasure hunt. Each car would rush to a compass bearing where an officer would issue another compass bearing and so on, each commander having to map read the route to the bearings. Unfortunately there was only one compass per officer and none for the crews. So we only got one look at the compass which the officer was holding. Gone was the comradeship – everybody calling

each other all the names under the sun as they struggled to get hold of the compass. Matters were not helped because there was only one gate through which to exit. The speed was a steady thirty with an umpire on each vehicle to see it was adhered to. But only one compass at each report point.

Another reflection on the social status of the officers and the unusual Yeomanry cama-raderie between officers and ORs was jotted down by the observant sergeant. In 1936 at Felixstowe, most of the 'troop leaders' (still strictly 'section leaders') had Rolls-Royce cars, the civilian variety, of their own. As the sections went out in their armoured cars, the lieutenants drove their civilian cars, taking 'crews' of troopers for an exhilarating change of steed.

By 1937 there was an ominous change in the type of training as the regiment went to its annual camp at Lulworth, part of the Royal Tank Corps headquarters and training area. The Rolls-Royces were not taken with them but the Territorials had to use the Lanchesters of the 12th Lancers, a regular unit. At first only the regulars drove the cars and there were mixed crews of regulars and Territorials, both officers and ORs. However, the more serious nature of training was relieved when a road march to Tidworth was laid on, enabling most of the Yeomen to see the famous annual Tidworth military tattoo. Later in the week on free time, a group of Yeomen made their way independently to Tidworth to see the tattoo, but did not have enough money to pay the entry fee for all the party. A quick-thinking corporal then lined the men up, marched them to the entry point, announced, 'fatigue party reporting for duty', and marched them through. Unfortunately, the days of 'fun and games' annual camps were at an end as Hitler was now moving into the offensive mode, having successfully taken over Austria and the Sudetenland virtually unopposed.

On 29 and 30 September 1938, in a conference at Munich, Britain and France had meekly agreed to Hitler's demand to be allowed to invade and occupy the Germanic Sudeten area of Czechoslovakia. The Czechoslovakians were not involved in the agree-ment and were powerless observers and victims of the greater nations. The armed forces of Britain were not ready for war and, essentially, the Munich Agreement allowed some measure of additional time for war preparation. With a politician's eye for diplomatic tri-umphs, the prime minister, Neville Chamberlain, flew back to Britain flourishing a piece of paper signed by Adolf Hitler, and giving the impression that this was 'peace in our time'. Many believed it and rejoiced. A considerable number, though, ranging from Sergeant George Jelley to Winston Churchill, did not. It was doubtful if Chamberlain himself was as naïve as he sounded, and in the event all the ministers of the armed forces departments immediately rushed ahead with plans to increase Britain's naval, military and air power.

Mr Leslie Hore-Belisha at the War Ministry disguised the first rush of conscription by describing the new conscripts as 'the Militiamen' – traditionally a type of service rather less than 'regular' and, in past times, limited to home defence. These were single men, ostensibly required to serve for only one year. In addition to their uniforms they also received a new civilian suit each. In fact the imminent outbreak of war meant that the militia was the first line of reinforcement to the regulars and the title 'Militiamen' there-fore soon disappeared. Meanwhile, the Yeomanry armoured car squadrons (RTC) were being re-established as full regiments, each consisting of three fighting squadrons and one

Reg Spittles at his wedding in traditional 'blues' with mail epaulets. *(Spittles)*

HQ squadron. They resumed their original titles as part of the Royal Armoured Corps (RAC), while the old Royal Tank Corps had become a separate elite tank regiment as the Royal Tank Regiment (RTR), divided into battalions.

In Lincolnshire, Fred Leary was among the first to be called up and labelled a Militiaman, although he would not remain a 'Lincolnshire Poacher' for very long. In Northampton, Reg Spittles would have been due to become a Militiaman but opted to join the Yeomanry Territorials before he was conscripted. Reg Spittles' main reason for choosing the Territorials was that after serving the due period as a Militiaman 'you would have lost your job. No employer would have kept your job open on your return. There was a thing called "unemployment" in the 20s and 30s. That's why 650 lads became the 2nd NY during April/May 1939. Simple!'

George Jelley was delighted to learn that he had been unexpectedly promoted to sergeant major and, taking off the three stripes on the upper sleeves and stitching on the crown above the cuffs, he reported to headquarters. 'I was told I was SSM of C Squadron.' George had never heard of a C Squadron and enquired where it was. The reply was, in effect, 'It isn't yet!' It was yet to be formed in Brackley. George, still doing a civilian job, was to form a squadron from recruits applying to Brackley Drill Hall. Arriving at Brackley, George had another surprise:

A lorry from Daventry duly arrived and, lo and behold, out tumbled a whole lorry load. Never had I seen so many men dismount from a lorry … My first parade state had been 1 Officer, 1 Warrant Officer (me) and 1 Sergeant. No troopers. One permanent staff (Royal Tank Corps regular) standing by to help training. One man from the Quartermaster's store available to issue clothing. Then the lorry load of men from Daventry and local recruits from Brackley. The first real parade in May 1939, ninety-three men all in civilian clothes. Next, I was told I must have my full complement of NCOs for the Annual Camp. With all respect to the professional soldier I could imagine him throwing up his hands in despair and saying 'Impossible! Ridiculous!'

George was told that, except for the single sergeant already available, all his sergeants, corporals and lance corporals had to come from his mixed batch of enthusiastic new-comers, all unknown quantities even though physically good-looking material. After a quick conference with his one officer, George asked if any of the volunteers had been members of the army cadets at school. Several had been, and these immediately became sergeants and corporals. The lance corporals came from others who either looked more experienced or who stood up straighter as they formed rather ragged ranks.

Hitler followed up the agreed occupation of part of Czechoslovakia a few months later by invading and taking over the rest of the country. Poland seemed to be the next prey for the Nazis' programme of *liebensraum*, or living space for German emigrants. Britain and France agreed to protect Poland if and when such an emergency arose. Most people now expected war and many young men decided to volunteer before being conscripted. Yeomanry regiments across the country, aiming to recruit to full regimental strength, found themselves inundated and able to contemplate forming two regiments rather than one.

In August 1939, SSM George Jelley assembled his three troops at Brackley and two troops at Daventry, for what was to be the last peacetime camp at Stockbridge, with 'not one squadron, not one regiment, but two regiments – all volunteers!' He went to Daventry to assemble the troops for the journey to Stockbridge and was astonished by the civic enthusiasm he found there:

> I found the market square full of people. Mostly children. On enquiring what the excitement was all about I was told that the Sqdn was going to march through the town. I asked 'Who said so?' No one seemed to know. And so we marched! Excuse me, did I say 'marched'? I had never seen anything like this march. Squealing children running in between the ranks. Parents, sweethearts and wives kissing loved ones and shouting greetings to those they knew, with the men themselves totally unused to this sort of thing. Enthusiasm everywhere. Flags waving ... And so the [Northants] Yeomanry went to camp in Stockbridge. Two regiments of volunteers out of one squadron a year ago. Why did they come? Well, once more someone was treading on the Lion's tail and, like their fathers, they wanted to know and do something about it.[3]

Within three weeks war had been declared. Overnight the part-time, volunteer Yeomen found themselves subjected to all the discipline, duties, skills and perils expected of any regular soldier. And George Jelley would proudly lead his men ashore on the Normandy beaches as the regimental sergeant major.

CHAPTER EIGHT

TWO LINES OF DEFENCE
(1939–1944)

Hastening preparations for the impending clash with the German war machine, the War Office doubled the establishment of the Territorial Army. This meant that Yeomanry regiments, most of them still well below war strength, would be required to recruit not just one full-strength regiment but two. The precipitate nature of affairs ensured that, battle ready or not, they would be mobilised immediately for active service. In traditional parlance the double regiments were known as 'the First Line' and 'the Second Line'. In the coming war this did not necessarily mean that the First Line would have a superior role to the Second Line or indeed that their roles would always be similar.

On 1 September 1939 Polish troops began to shoot back as the German army defied the ultimata of the British and French governments and continued their push for further territory. On 3 September 1939 Britain and France declared war and the British dominions followed suit. Poland resisted for almost three weeks before being invaded by Soviet Russia on 17 September and, although the nation never formally surrendered, its forces withdrew to neutral Romania. Britain was left helpless in respect of its promises to Poland but, having now made a determined enemy of Hitler, needed to gain a full war footing without further delay.

On 1 September 1939, Corporal, Acting Sergeant A.E. 'Sandy' Saunders reported to Kettering Drill Hall. Correction: in mid-August Corporal, Acting Sergeant A.E. Saunders had received his calling-up papers, but on arrival at Kettering Drill Hall found himself already to be Second Lieutenant Saunders. Just as George Jelley was creating instant sergeants and corporals, officers were being commissioned urgently from the ranks. Troop Sergeant Major Tom Boardman also became a second lieutenant virtually overnight. Sandy Saunders was further surprised to be told that there was no room for officers, or indeed for many of the ORs in the Drill Hall, and was sent back to billet at his own house, to 'a rapturous welcome' from his wife for the returning hero. Among the ORs, B and C Squadrons shared sleeping at home duties on a rota for weeks, while finding the men something to do was equally chaotic:

> We practised Troop formations on foot across the playing fields alongside Kettering Railway Station, a chaos of small bodies of men in line abreast, line ahead, arrowhead, and so on, changing our formations by whistle and hand signals! And sometimes even

joined in groups by holding lengths of string. It was all called TEWTs, tank exercises without tanks. This happy, if shambolic start to our WAR lasted until October when, in turn, the Squadrons took guard duties at RAF Wyton.[1]

Such were Sandy's impressions of the Second Line as Lieutenant Colonel Prior Palmer and his few well-trained helpers worked to achieve discipline and order. The First Line was having similar experiences, in spite of the best efforts of Lieutenant Colonel A.F.G. Renton, commanding. Several Buckinghamshire lads, including Jack Aris, had crossed the border to Brackley to join local friends in the Territorials. Now they found themselves constituted as C Squadron, 1NY. To their delight the local Drill Hall was too small and many of the rankers were billeted in the upper floors of local pubs. In Daventry a dilapidated hotel, the Peacock, offered shelter. However, C Squadron had no cook and so at the first parade an urgent appeal was made, 'Anybody here know how to cook?' There was a long silence. Eventually, jovial Jack Aris raised a hand and stated rather nervously, 'I used to serve the packet sandwiches in the factory canteen'. In spite of laughter from his mates the qualification was sufficient: Jack was appointed cook corporal on the spot. He would become famous for his 'rainbow rice' – ordinary rice but dignified by whatever coloured ingredient could be introduced without poisoning the troops, custard powder, paprika, gentian violet or, some said, soot. C Squadron, after various TEWTs, found itself guarding railway tunnels on the main line, as the lads joked: 'Just in case Jerry comes and pinches the tunnels.' A more bureaucratic view was 'danger of saboteurs' as rumours abounded of German paratroopers descending dressed as policemen or nuns.

Meanwhile on 12 December 1939 the Northants squadrons found themselves reinforced by a considerable draft of Lincolnshire Militiamen, like Percy Epton and Fred Leary. The merger of original Territorials and other reinforcements had begun and would continue unabated during the war. Neither Percy nor Fred had ever left Lincolnshire before in their lives, but now the poachers, fishermen and farmers would merge with the shoemakers and brewers to form a fertile broth of comradeship and energy. What has become known as the 'phoney war' of inactivity had bogged down the battle lines between France and Germany but there would eventually be need for reinforcements, both there and in other battle zones not yet initiated. The Yeomanry regiments were being given their roles for future developments, although few soldiers as yet anticipated the terrible catastrophe which would occur in the spring, an event remembered in Britain simply as 'Dunkirk'. For Fred Leary it was a cultural shock, being sent to a luxurious country estate, Wooton Hall, but faced with the most basic conditions:

A corporal counted out eight lads to each room – no beds, just bare boards and two blankets. We were forbidden to use the bathrooms which were for officers only. We had a contraption in the park, a shed without a front, open to elements and only cold water. No real army vehicles. A collection of second-hand cars sprayed with camouflage paint. A black van with Air France written on it. A small Bedford bus. Each morning we went down to an improvised parade ground where the drill sergeant shouted insults at us. But Corporal [later Sergeant Reg] King was a great help to us rookies. He came in the evening and would sit on our beds and talk like a father on how to make the best of army life. [2]

The two lines of Northants learned that they would be similarly equipped with light tanks and armoured cars and would operate together with another Yeomanry regiment from Gloucestershire. This was not a common experience for Yeomanry in general, the two lines twinned in Home Defence and then serving on into Normandy. Most of the counties who succeeded in forming two lines found that they were to split, both in terms of armament and location. One line of the Royal Gloucester Hussars would, at first, be brigaded with the two Northants regiments whilst the other RGH line would have a different role. Similarly, the 1st and 2nd Derbyshire Yeomanry would have separate destinies in different divisions. Both the 1st and 2nd Fife and Forfar and the 1st and 2nd Lothian Border would have separate paths and eventually considerably different armament and battle purposes. [3]

A number of Yeomanry regiments, like the Leicesters, were now armed as field artillery. The two Leicester lines would be known as 153rd and 154th Field Regiments, Royal Artillery, maintaining their traditional designation within brackets, but would have widely varying travels with their guns. Some regiments, such as the Wiltshires, Warwickshires and Cheshires, were delighted to learn that they would be retaining their cherished horses, but the good news was tempered by an early despatch of those units to places like Palestine, Egypt, Persia and Syria.

To begin with, the larger picture meant little to the newly mobilised young soldiers. Among the most important considerations were the smartness of the uniform for walking out with girls and the sanctity of the regimental badge. As a Territorial, Reg Spittles brought with him the normal service dress of a full-length khaki tunic with brass

Cheshire Yeomanry still mounted, Syria, in 1941, just before the last horses were withdrawn from service. *(Cheshire Yeo Museum and, IWM E3593)*

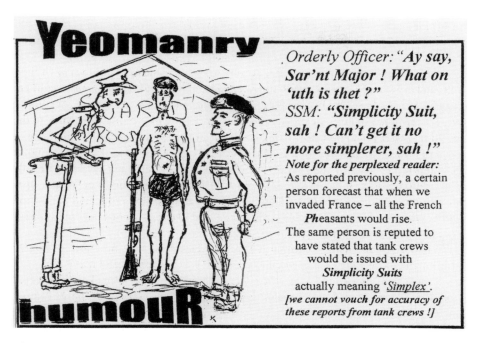

The cartoon refers to the issue of the one-piece Simplex tank suit, which the sergeant major could not pronounce. *(Tout, NYA)*

buttons and a beret, as well as a smart blue walking-out uniform, with silver chain metal epaulets (in which he would proudly get married) and a swagger stick to carry. Around him he saw new recruits hurriedly issued with boiler suits for the time being. It was two months before full uniform and military underwear were issued, not that Reg enjoyed the change to the latter, the new underpants and vests being 'thick and very tickly'. The regimental badge was the galloping 'White Horse of Hanover' within a scroll bearing the regiment's name. Unfortunately the number of badges in stock was sufficient for only one regiment. The colonels conferred and, after tossing a coin, 2NY took possession of the cap badge. The 1NY had to make do with the simple silver horse, normally the collar dog, on a blue cloth patch. Later a new colonel changed 2NY headdress to a side cap, but later still they reverted to the Royal Armoured Corps black beret.

Confusion became nationwide when, in the spring of 1940, the massed German armour, profiting from new tactics and using close air support, broke through the Allied armies, causing the eventual surrender of the French Army and the evacuation of the British, with some Allied soldiers, from Dunkirk. More than one Yeomanry fought well in an impossible situation: 1st Lothian and Border Yeomanry carried out a 60-mile fighting retreat over six days and survived to fight again; the Worcesters with their guns defended the approaches to Dunkirk itself until ordered to detach and evacuate.

Virtually within a month the picture had changed from dormant armies facing each other across frontiers well away from Britain to an enemy standing at Calais and looking across the sea to the iconic white cliffs. The same enemy was assembling landing craft and massing aircraft for an invasion of England, unthinkable only a few weeks previously.

And the evacuated army was completely disorganised for the time being. Major Bill Close MC and bar related how the remnants of his regiment, 3RTR, evacuated from Calais and were sent to patrol the south coast of England with 'no tanks, very few vehicles and just Boyes rifles, an extremely difficult weapon, in fact quite useless'.[4]

Suddenly, partially trained and equipped troops like the NY were needed as emergency plugs for a hurried defence line along the threatened coast. Reg Spittles' squadron boasted two Rolls-Royce armoured cars, one old light Vickers tank and half a dozen trucks. Reg and Freddy Wilson manned a requisitioned 5-ton furniture lorry which carried all the quartermaster supplies. A selection of reasonably trained soldiers of 1 and 2NY and RGH were formed into the Yeomanry Armoured Detachment (YAD), as an urgent front-line group of one regiment strength. However, the strategist Kenneth Macksey, in his study of what would have happened if the enemy had landed in July 1940, places the two Northants regiments and the Gloucesters as one out of only two armoured brigades available for immediate counterattack against the incoming enemy. And Reg's old Vickers tank at a 7-ton weight would have been facing enemy armour of 20 tons or more and with much bigger guns.[5]

It is difficult to recreate the atmosphere of 1940 in Britain. The government launched campaigns to warn about possible enemy spies, whilst loudly proclaiming the incarceration of a multitude of suspect enemy aliens. Posters screamed 'Walls have ears' or 'Be like Dad, keep Mum!' Signposts and name plates were removed from roads and railway stations. Campanologists were preparing to ring the alarm on church bells and the code word 'Cromwell' was circulated as the signal that the enemy had landed. Indeed, rumour had it that some enemy troops had actually come ashore and been consumed in an oily fire. Post-war research has denied that story, but a Pioneer Corps man showed patrolling Reg Spittles a handful of German tunic buttons from bodies which his unit had buried by the beach after an abortive landing. Whom to believe?

As with the 1794 Yeomanry, Britain now formed a Home Guard of part-time volunteers to guard the homeland. One of the first volunteers in Northampton was George Dixon, the 1914–18 diarist. Johnny Howell, 17 years old and later a 1NY trooper, proudly wore his LDV armband as he guarded a railway arch in Dorset. He was not too impressed by their secret weapon, a 40-gallon drum filled with inflammable liquid which they were to spray via a hand pump on to approaching German tanks. True to Yeomanry tradition, the Yorkshire County Hunt volunteered to bring their horses to Home Guard service in order to spot German parachutists, calling themselves 'The Parashots', according to the *Daily Sketch*.

Bill Moseley, a Northants Yeoman on a course at Bovington, was paraded with several other students and told to man a venerable relic, an experimental tank called the 'Independent', stored in what would become the famous Bovington Tank Museum. It had a huge engine which needed six men to start it. It boasted five turrets but with nothing larger than machine guns. And fatally, even once its engine had been bullied into starting, it could not be made to move. It was towed down to the cliffs above Lulworth and set up as an extempore fort, where Bill was appointed signaller. His contact was an officer on an opposite cliff. There was no wireless, so the officer had a heliograph with which, if the sun was up and in the right direction, he could send da–dit–dit–dit / dit–dah–dit / dah–dah–dah, / etc. to spell Cromwell.

At the highest level of government there was concern as to what would happen if the Germans reached London with the king still at Buckingham Palace or Windsor Castle. And what about the beloved queen and princesses? The king was persuaded that, at a certain point, he must go to Canada which had vowed to fight on after the demise of the mother country. The King's Company of the Grenadier Guards could protect the royal family in their palaces, but what would happen en route between Windsor and the port of departure in Liverpool, given the possibility of enemy infiltrators?

Lieutenant Colonel Prior Palmer of 2NY was instructed to select a subaltern of impeccable manners and utmost efficiency, together with a troop of cars manned by NCOs and troopers of a similar character, for a top-secret mission, code-named 'COATS'. The instructions were so precise and imperative that Prior Palmer was able to make an educated guess as to what was afoot. He selected Lieutenant M.J.M. Humblecroft and suitable crews for four Guy 'wheeled tanks'. Heading to an anonymous rendezvous and being redirected, the troop found itself entering Windsor Castle. There they were teamed up with a similar troop of the 12th Lancers (Lieutenant Morris) and a company of the Coldstream Guards under a Lieutenant Ian Liddell, who later in the war died whilst winning the Victoria Cross. The group was commanded by Major Jimmy Coats, hence the name of the mission.

The king called the tiny convoy 'my private army'. Two armoured cars of each troop would be fitted with comfortable seats in the turret, while the other two cars would be munitioned to battle standard. The Lancers would carry the king, or if he refused to go at that juncture, the queen and aides, and the NY cars would carry the two princesses. So for a time Lieutenant Humblecroft, Sergeant Paul Curtis and crews had the delight of driving Princess Elizabeth and Princess Margaret Rose around Windsor on test exercises. Fortunately the Coats mission was never needed as the Germans were defeated in the Battle of Britain and the invasion was postponed indefinitely on 17 September 1940. It is not thought that the gunners in the two adapted NY cars were allowed to retain the comfortable chairs designed for the princesses.

Other men or small groups were suddenly despatched to various sideshows of the greater strategic war. Six NY men including Trooper Tom Cooper, later a lieutenant, were attached to a reconnaissance and signals unit (with an 'independent company', later commando) 'somewhere in England', put aboard the *Ulster Princess* at Leith and, on Whit Monday 1940, found themselves going ashore in Norway at Bodo, 'a beautiful small fishing port with coloured wooden houses set on stone foundations'. The group was known as 'The Scissors', placed between two larger British landings, an abortive expedition intended to prevent the Germans from taking over Norway. Tom Cooper reflected:

We were housed at first in a large red barn which contained the rear HQ wireless link back to London. We were issued with French police Mauser pistols, American gangster type 'Tommy guns' and, more important, warm wool-lined parkas. We had no sooner reached the forward HQ than the army withdrew. L/Cpl Crippin found an abandoned motor cycle and that saved our boots on the journey back to Bodo. During our absence beautiful Bodo had been bombed completely and only the stone foundations of the wooden houses remained. We embarked on a destroyer whose superstructure was badly chopped about. Travelled to the island of Harstad. We were transhipped in mid ocean to the Lancastria. And eventually arrived back in Gourrock. After a short period in Arisaig and Lochailort we moved to Lands End, England with a zone including the Scillies before I was sent back to the NY.

After his purposeless adventure in an abortive trek around remote northern locations, Tom Cooper might have thought that the war had given him enough surprises. He was not to know that, after being commissioned, he would eventually be attached to the Madras Guards.

From within the two NY regiments, as the threat of invasion receded, trained men were now being despatched to the Middle and Near East where other Yeomanry regiments, horsed or motorised, were already in action. Officers in particular arrived and, after a day or a week or a month, departed usually to unknown destinations overseas. Over about two years the NY contributed more than sixty officers to the Middle East war, a number in excess of its own total officer strength, and ORs were similarly drafted in considerable numbers. Territorials like George Jelley, Reg Spittles, Sandy Saunders and Jack Aris, and early arrivals like Fred Leary, formed a continuing firm spine of experience and tradition. In effect all soldiers from all types of recruitment were now 'regulars'. They watched and waited as Reg remembers:

> Of course we were unhappy to lose good mates. One day you would be soldiering with someone and tripping over them in the tent, and the next day they were packing up and disappearing for ever, almost without notice. Some officers you never even learned their names. I was happy not to be sent as I was arranging to get married. Of course we had joined up to fight for our country and wanted to do something more than just training and drilling. But we knew that at some time our turn would come and, in any case, until that day there was not very much you could do about it, knowing so little about what was really going on.

One of the most unusual assignments involved Sergeant Reg King (later MM) also of 2NY, who was ordered to go home and fetch his civilian clothes. On call up as a Territorial he had been promoted three times in quick succession, 'the blind leading the blind' as he says, and his first sergeant's task was to mark out bed spaces for an entire regiment on the floor of Northampton Drill Hall. He was then sent on a promotion course to the Guards Depot at Caterham and promoted again to warrant officer grade 3 (WOIII). Within a short time the War Office abolished that rank and that of troop sergeant major, so Reg reverted to troop sergeant and was sent home for his clothes:

> 40 sergeants, WO's and officers were, under great secrecy, kitted out with civilian clothes, issued with passports as British Government employees and sent up to the Clyde, on a troop ship full of RAF going to CANADA for flying training. I was in a group with Maj Peter Grant (1NY), Capt R.H. Courage (2NY), Capt John Profumo (1NY), Capt Robinson (15/19th Lancers), a captain from 2RGH and 2 from 2RTR. We went to Halifax, Nova Scotia, where we at last learned what we were to do. We went by train to Washington, DC, and ultimately to ***Fort Knox, Kentucky, USA*** to tell the Americans what kind of Armoured Fighting Vehicle would suit the British

Army, under the Lease/Lend Act. The fact is: we were largely responsible for helping the Americans (who had no recent experience of tank warfare) to arrive at the final SHERMAN TANK design. We then went back to Camp Borden, Ontario, Canada to help train instructors on the tanks and guns that would come from the USA. Then eventually back to Blighty.

Meanwhile, away in the Middle East, the reign of the horsed Yeoman was coming to a gradual end. If King George III had needed 10,000 horses to defend his kingdom, King George VI needed none in the front line. Even up to 1941 Yeomanry regiments had rendered good service while horsed in wide, open regions against scattered foes. Now the command came to hand in their cherished horses and learn the mysteries of battle while riding noisy machines powered by the internal combustion engine. It was 1942 before the proud Cheshire Yeomanry dismounted and had imposed on them the prosaic title of 5th Lines of Communications Signals Regiment. Did they remember that one of their officers, the Duke of Westminster, adapted the prototype of the Rolls-Royce armoured car at his own expense in 1914?

The two NY regiments were still brigaded together with 2RGH and shared many common experiences of training in larger formations on 'schemes'. Much of the routine was still on a peacetime basis and the extent of 'bullshit' depended on the colonel. The 2NY found popular Prior Palmer promoted and a new colonel, D.A.R.B. Cooke, a traditional cavalryman, in charge. In Reg Spittles' words, the new colonel's philosophy was 'if it moves shoot it. If it doesn't move, paint it.' Sandy Saunders was astonished to be told to polish the 'unpolishable' gunmetal buttons on his greatcoat. Fred Leary gradually adapted to the routine:

Very often the four squadrons camped apart within a radius of about three miles. A few times we would all be in one camp such as Ogbourne [Wiltshire] or Beverley. At these times there would be a twenty-four hour guard, known as a 'quarter guard'. The guard was mounted at 09.00 hours with a certain amount of ceremony. The officer of the day would inspect the thirteen men of the new guard. Why thirteen men? Because the 'best turned out man', in the officer's opinion, would be given the 'stick', not on his hand as in school days, but a 'swagger stick'. Meaning he could run a few errands for the RSM and finish his duty at 12.00 hours. The rest of the men would be on duty until 09.00 next morning. So it was worth a bit of effort to win 'stick man'. Not so easy if your only way of creasing trousers was laying them out under your bedding on the ground and sleeping on them overnight.[6]

At this time the army was calling up 18-year-old men to be given initial training and be posted to various military tasks, many of them becoming the tank crews for the D-Day campaign and thereafter, often commanded by the old Territorials as NCOs. No real choice was offered on registering for call up and the boy might be directed to navy, army, air force or even to compulsory work down a coal mine, also known as the 'Bevin Boys'. Once within the army the choice was again limited. When Stan Hicken was asked what regiment he would like to join he replied: 'The Warwickshire Yeomanry' (his home unit). He was told: 'They are overseas and you are too young to go overseas' and was sent to the Northants. At first Stan's ideas about the army were rather naïve and he would soon learn that the old attitudes died fast:

> Roy Gadsby and I had been selected by our squadron leader as potential officers, so one day we were sent for an interview. I went in first and there was this purple-faced major (not NY) sitting there and he was quite insulting. The first thing he asked me was 'Do you ride a horse?' So I said I could but I didn't much care for it. He said, 'Oh! So your father's a stationmaster, isn't he?' I said 'No, he's a special relief man – does any job, including stationmaster'. The officer replied 'So if you ran up a mess bill and couldn't pay it, would he be in a position to pay it for you?' I felt he was just out to insult my father. That didn't go down well with me. And obviously I didn't go down well with him. I heard no more about being an officer.[7]

In October 1942 in the Western Desert the crucial Second Battle of El Alamein took place and several Yeomanry units revealed that they were fit to stand with the best of regular units. An old Yeomanry cavalry brigade had now become the 8th Armoured Brigade, with their horses exchanged for Crusader, Grant and Sherman tanks. These were crewed by the Sherwood Rangers (Notts Yeomanry), Staffordshire Yeomanry and an RTR battalion with the Kent Yeomanry as artillery. Similarly, the 9th Armoured Brigade had the Royal Wilts and Warwickshires now in tanks, joined by the 3rd Hussars with the Middlesex Yeomanry in a signals role. In advancing against elite enemy troops like the 15th and 21st Panzers, the brigades performed heroically, suffering considerable casualties but launching the great advance through Benghazi and Tripoli and eventually on to Sicily and mainland Italy.

In England the pleasant association of the two Northants regiments with their Gloucester comrades was about to end. Planning was continuing for a 'Second Front' landing in France to relieve the Russians who were under tremendous pressure on the Eastern Front. The three regiments were still stationed in adjacent locations near the Marlborough Downs. The 2NY had become notable for the 'shoot it or paint it' regime of Lieutenant Colonel Cooke, not always popular with the men who had to paint the same stones time and time again. There were universal plaudits, therefore, for the lorry driver who managed to crash into the highly decorated sentry box, smashing it to pieces and scattering some of the colonel's sacred stones. The lorry driver subsequently learned new and colourful terms of endearment.

Whilst the First and Second NY Lines, Siamese twins until now, prepared to separate and differentiate, a 4th Northamptonshire Yeomanry was suddenly and quietly invented. Throughout the war British tactics had included a considerable input of deception, misleading the enemy as to future intentions. A deception officer named David Strangeways was told to convince Turkey that the Allies had forces in nearby Iraq, the purpose being to keep Turkey from joining Germany in the war. With a few operators and two radio sets he simulated an entire regimental programme of messages from his fictional 4NY close to the border, on which the Turks could eavesdrop. Strangeways later invented 'the man who never was', an officer's body floated ashore in Spain. The 1NY's Sergeant Dick 'Bandy' Spicer would himself be posted to a similar deception unit in preparation for D-Day 1944.

The question of the 'Second Front' was now looming high in the thoughts of both the high commanders and the troopers. Lieutenant Colonel W. A. Howkins, NY, had been disappointed to be medically downgraded due to a serious hearing problem. After various promotions he was appointed Secretary to the Joint Planning Staff of Britain and America, and in this capacity attended and did much of the organising of the Casablanca Conference. There Roosevelt and Churchill, in the absence of Stalin who was supervising the critical Stalingrad battle, decided that the Second Front would not take place in the summer of 1943 but in 1944. Thereafter sent to Washington, one important element of Howkins' role was to plan the way in which civil affairs would be handled by the military as the armies advanced into enemy countries.

At a far more humble level, the residents of quiet Stow-cum-Quy village near Cambridge were awakened by something like a tropical storm: thundering engines, flashing backfires and huge clouds of dust along a narrow lane. The 2NY had arrived with their new heavier tanks, Valentines and Matildas, which replaced the lighter vehicles of YAD days. Arnold Morley, 8 years old at the time and like little Bertie Taylor forty years earlier, decided that these new machines must be investigated. Borrowing an old wheelbarrow, Arnold and pal Jimmy Taylor approached the NY sentry and demanded citizens' rights to collect old newspapers for the war salvage effort. This was referred to the corporal of the guard and on to more eminent authorities, such as RSM Kenward. Like Bertie of old, Arnold and Jimmy got their contract to collect old newspapers daily, with suitable bonuses whenever passing the cookhouse.

Despite not directly confronting the enemy, life around tanks could be dangerous at times. Just before Christmas 1942 1NY went to 75mm cannon practice at Linney Head ranges, on the historic Castlemartin Yeomanry preserves. Lieutenant Godby commanded one of the tanks where a corporal, acting as gun loader, somehow caught his wedding ring in the open gun mechanism and the shell jammed. Before any misfire action could be taken the shell exploded, blowing off the loader's hand. The full impact of the explosion caught the lieutenant who was killed instantaneously. In another accident, on a very steep hill in Gloucester, the brakes of a tank suddenly failed. It ran down the incline, knocking over and killing two men, Trooper Len Webb and Lance Corporal Charles Doger de Speville, the latter being a barrister-at-law who had come from the Seychelles to join up and was awaiting a commission. The two NY lines lost seventeen men in England due to accidents or exposure-related illnesses.

Such pre-battle losses may have encouraged several NY colonels and majors to assemble at the Ritz Hotel, London, in 1943, not for convivial purposes, but to discuss extending the 1930s Old Comrades Association into a new trust to care for soldiers of the current war. The Earl Spencer of the day took the chair and much discussion centred on whether such provision should be available only for those who fought wearing the regimental badge, or whether it might include the considerable number of men who passed through the regiment but fought wearing other badges. In the event the crucial criterion of service in the NY 'at any time' won the day.

Meanwhile, the routine continued with large-scale schemes, further training courses and visits to firing ranges – the latter with a rota as varied as peacetime camps: Linney Head, Dunwich, Titchwell, Lulworth, Warcop. The first heavier tanks, such as old Matildas, Valentines and Crusaders, gave way to bigger, faster and more reliable

Cromwells (2NY) and Shermans (1NY). Gunners and loaders were assured that all that was British (or American lease-loaned) was best; and were not yet fully aware of the thicker armament on the front of Panthers and Tigers, or the better guns on even the smaller German Mk IV. Nor had they yet looked inside a burned-out Sherman tank. Higher authorities were only too aware of British deficiencies but, as the posters admonished the public, the military generals also 'kept mum'.

D-Day 1944 was approaching, although not yet known to troopers by that code word. In May 1944 the author, with nineteen other gunners, was loaded on to a 3-ton lorry and taken away to a 'secret destination' under strict orders of silence. The vehicle travelled from near Bury St Edmunds to the Brancaster/Titchwell area on the Norfolk coast. The driver was directed up a dirt road to a belt of trees on a hill top, a place of Druid aura, dark and mysterious. Rounding a corner they discovered a Sherman tank hidden in the trees, but it was a Sherman with a difference. This was the Firefly with a greatly extended, larger gun, pointing at the moment out to sea towards a sunken ship about 2,500 yards away, far beyond normal tank gun range. The gunners were informed that, because of shortage of ammunition and concern about wearing out the gun barrel, each man would load only one round and then, with someone else loading, fire only one round at the sunken ship. They thus became gunners qualified to fire a 17-pounder, which would prove to be a better gun than those carried by Panthers and Tigers: a veritable secret weapon.

Perhaps the author might be permitted to include a glimpse upwards from a gunner's seat to describe a trooper's view of a fairly typical yeomanry regiment ready for D-Day. The 1NY's Lieutenant Colonel Doug Forster, a surname not unknown in the racing world, was a quiet, unobtrusive regular cavalryman, recently retired in 1939 but recalled to command. He rarely raised his voice and was content to let his squadron leaders command in their own distinctive ways. Perhaps surprisingly, from a trooper's viewpoint, he was known to his cavalry peers as 'a hard rider to hounds'.

Of the four majors only one was a regular officer: C Squadron leader, Territorial, or 'War Substantive' Maj. David 'Hank' Bevan had passed through the famous playing fields of Eton, and was a tall, young, charismatic figure, usually remote from the troopers but when required to talk face to face was pleasant and just. He had enlisted and been commissioned early and so was senior to his second-in-command, who was several years older. The second-in-command, Captain Bill Fox, was a total contrast, able to decorate the English language with variations previously unheard, and was a bareback rider reputed to have been a cavalry trooper and American cowboy. His wrinkled, mobile face, quick to show displeasure but slow to display rancour, revealed unexpected signs of bereavement when casualties occurred. The second captain, Michael 'Ratters' Rathbone, carried his school nickname for he had taught several rankers at a Brackley school and still maintained a schoolmasterly attitude to command.

There were five lieutenants, two of them younger than most of the troopers, Bobby McColl and Tony Faulkner. Although inexperienced, they both proved excellent commanders, the former a taciturn Scot, the latter an extrovert 'good chap'. The subalterns were generally given due respect, except for one who assumed a supercilious attitude and put more people on charges than the other four combined. Soldiers were quick to resent an officer who showed pretensions which might be described as 'above his station'.

The sergeant and corporals, who were the tank commanders and administrators, were almost all original Territorials. Having now worn uniform full time for five years, they could be counted as professional soldiers. The author's then troop sergeant, Dick Bates, an elderly, florid-faced jovial man, had been a nobleman's chauffeur in peacetime and was more of an uncle to the 19- and 20-year-olds than a commander. The troop corporal, however, seemed to resent the lack of high-visibility discipline around him and compensated by becoming the strictest martinet among the daily contacts. The vast majority of the inside crews were about 20 years of age and had been through a rigid and adequate technical training for their tasks. Many of them had been selected for tank crew training as a result of IQ and aptitude testing which were still quite novel at the time.

Probably the two most important people in the regiment were the RSM and one's own SSM. In 1NY the RSM was now the redoubtable George Jelley, who had the advantage of having been a boy soldier in the previous war. He therefore thoroughly comprehended the problems and attitudes of his young charges. A big man both in physique and voice, he had the further advantage of being an enthusiastic football referee and the sight of his muscular knees on the football field made it easier to realise that he was a human being, a term not always applied by rankers to RSMs. He could shout at a range of a hundred yards if required, but could also personally thank troopers for their excellent turn out after a brigadier's inspection.

SSM Sid Turton, aged 30, was a physical contrast to George, smaller, unbelievably neat at all times in all conditions, a whippet of a man, alternatively snapping at people's heels and then indulging in sardonic humour. He had spent time in a tuberculosis sanatorium as a sickly child but fought his way to fitness, joining the cavalry and becoming a staff sergeant before transfer to the 1NY as one of only two regular soldiers in the squadron of about 150 men. He perfected that strange relationship with rankers which distinguish his type, as Stan Hicken vividly remembered:

Our Squadron Sergeant Major had a fantastic sense of humour. I must tell you more about Sid Turton. One day Bill Rawlins and I were walking from our Nissen huts across the park to the tank aprons when, coming in the opposite direction we met Sid. As we approached he snapped 'Come on there! Smarten yourselves up! Try and look like soldiers!' So we swung our arms and straightened our shoulders a bit. After about ten yards he stopped behind us, turned round and said. 'I know what you are thinking. But you are wrong. I knew both my mother and father. And they WERE married. And take those bloody grins off your faces!' But he could not stand fools or slackness.

May 1944 arrived and destiny began to call, preceded by those military harbingers of real action, the censoring of letters home and a forty-seven-hour leave pass. When gunners tested their newly arrived 17-pounder Firefly variants, one to each three 75mm Shermans in a troop, they quickly discovered a fault with the cocking mechanism. A despatch rider was called, loaded with a case full of cocking mechanisms and ordered to speed on his motorbike from Bury St Edmunds to a factory in South Wales to have the items checked and altered. On return the despatch rider would find the regiment moved to an Aldershot staging point and lodged in Guards accommodation in Mons Lines. The 2NY also began the move towards the docks and 'hards' of the south coast.

Stan Hicken was the unwilling participant in the next hurried and obnoxious task, waterproofing newly delivered Duplex-Drive (DD) tanks which were designed to traverse through the open sea:

> There was a top panic to get all our tanks waterproofed. This involved fitting big metal exhaust chutes at the back, fitting Macintosh (canvas) surrounds around the gun ports and any other holes, like the fuel cap; and all cracks and joins in the structure had to be sealed with funny black sticky plastic stuff (Bostik) which stuck to hands, overalls and boots and had to be painfully scraped off. The canvas Macintosh over the gun port was resting on a cradle of cortex and a fuse, so as soon as we got out of the sea we could fire the cortex fuse and blow the Macintosh off ready for action. We had then to take the tank to a lake and dip it in to test it. Any leaks? Put on more Bostik! All for inspection parade at nine next morning, working in daylight and dark.

Finally, out of the goodness of his heart, the resident Guards RSM, he of the thousand-decibel voice, decided to entertain the Yeomen by arranging a special drill parade *a la* Grenadiers, shouted by himself from distances almost as far as a 17-pounder's range, on the vast Mons parade ground. The Yeomen, who had been doing final maintenance and waterproofing tanks with Bostick, had lately been spared such drill exercises. Now they went through the entire routine of parading, ordering arms, advancing and retreating, quick march and slow march, until eventually they were required, in long line abreast, to march off in the general direction of the North Pole. Each trooper, terrified by the immense bulk and roaring voice of the RSM, sweated as they marched on and on with no reversing word of command, each fearful that, with the clatter of hundreds of boots, they might have failed to hear the Grenadier's final faint 'Halt!' Later the RSM smiled and paid the Yeomen the ultimate seal of approval, 'Not bad, seeing they are not Guardsmen'.

Released from the Grenadier RSM's clutches into the rather more genial care of George Jelley and the SSMs, the squadrons then paraded afresh, one by one, officers and men, in ranks six deep and mounted up in tiers on chairs and table tops. This was to be for the military equivalent of the condemned man's last meal: the squadron photograph.

CHAPTER NINE

ARMOURED STEEDS HUNT TIGERS
(1944–1946)

'There cannot be a more various organisation than that of the British Yeomanry Corps,' stated a publication of 1844.[1] This was never more strikingly illustrated than in the line-up of Yeomanry regiments in queues across much of southern England, waiting to load on to landing ships in June just 100 years later.

Even the two Northants lines had diverged in their role and equipment: the First manned Sherman tanks in the independent 33rd Armoured Brigade (three tank regiments available to work with infantry as required); the Second had the rather lighter, faster Cromwells as the reconnaissance unit for the 11th Armoured Division, the 'Charging Bull'. Whilst these tanks could wade ashore in a depth of water up to the hulls, the Staffordshire and the East Riding Yeomanry had special Duplex-Drive (DD) tanks which could swim in deep water.

Other Yeomanry regiments were even more diversified. Some were now mobile artillery using varied types of guns: the Ayrshires and several others were Field Regiments, RA; the Duke of Lancasters had medium guns; and the Northumberlands worked as anti-tank. In the specialist 79th Armoured Division, with its so-called 'Funnies', were the 1st Lothian and Border and 2nd County of London on mine-sweeping 'Crabs' with their front chains flailing the ground; the 1st Fife and Forfar used fearsome flame-throwing tanks, the 'Crocodiles'; the Inns of Court had armoured cars at Corps HQ; and the Cheshires formed Lines of Communications signals. Moving into the air, the Worcesters were now the 53rd Air Landing Light Regiment whilst the North Somersets served as Air Formation Signals. In times of need the army obviously turned to the Yeomanry for versatility.

The D-Day plan was to capture the pivotal large city of Caen on the first day, 6 June. The Staffordshire Yeomanry led the charge, swimming ashore and advancing in good time in spite of casualties. However, the enemy around Caen remained defiant for a whole month until a major RAF raid destroyed the defences of the city. Also on D-Day, one battery of the Worcesters took part in the successful parachute and glider landing attacks, which seized a vital bridge across the river north of Caen.

The build-up of troops continued across the beaches for weeks. The entire 1NY regiment crossed as a unit, although two squadrons of 2NY preceded the remainder of that regiment. From the moment of landing everyone was under fire in those first weeks after D-Day, and casualties were suffered. C Squadron, 1NY's Lieutenant Haskard and his tank had been requisitioned by the corps commander as his personal 'eyes and ears'. Rounding a random corner just off the beaches, the Sherman found itself face to face with a much more powerful German Panther. There was not time even for a token shot as the Panther gunner had been waiting for the Sherman. John Haskard, age 20, and his gunner, Bill Shellam, age 21, became the first NY men to die in Normandy. The 2NY experience was even more brutal.

Reg Spittles was now troop corporal of 2 Troop, A Squadron, under Major Bobby Peel, and his orders were to go forward and survey bridges over the River Odon. Early on 26 June they pushed forward into Cheux which had been heavily bombed. The water tower had been destroyed and the streets were a chaos of floods, thick mud and mounded rubble, enough to break the track of an unwary tank. As they clawed and slewed their way through Cheux the news came over the air that Captain Wyvill Raynsford, their second-in-command, had been killed by a sniper. 'Our first casualty, this was a great shock as he was a very popular officer and had been with the regiment since 1939.' Reg was to see and hear worse news still:

Being held in reserve I was able to observe no 3 Troop going up a cornfield at about 35mph, exactly like an exercise in England as though there was no enemy. At such speed no commander would have chance to observe forward. I looked away. In a few moments I looked back. They had reached the top of the hill but two of their three Cromwell tanks had already been destroyed and were burning like two haystacks on fire, thick black smoke billowing out. You can imagine the shock to my nervous system. So that was what happened to tanks? But no time to waste because Bobby Peel came on the radio and said 'Hullo 2 (that's us), get up there and see what's happened'. My troop leader, Lt Hobson on my radio just said '2 Baker (that's me) – lead!'

Reg started off more cautiously at about 15mph but was told by his lieutenant, 'Get a bloody move on!' He passed through the smoke between the two burning tanks to get some cover. Looking down from the hill he saw a convoy of enemy tanks crossing the valley, led by Panther tanks, followed by about twenty of the lighter Mk IVs (but still more powerful than the Cromwells) plus half-track carriers full of infantry and all going at speed. Reg's crew had some consolation as they hit and halted four of the Mk IVs but the enemy convoy sped on and out of sight (to meet a larger British attack which took place elsewhere). Reg then turned about and started picking up the wounded from 3 Troop. Radio messages confirmed that the 4 Troop tanks of Lieutenant Alex Stock (later renowned in the football world) and Sergeant Reg King (of the USA Sherman design team) had completed the bridge survey. They were all ordered to return to Cheux, where they found a burial party interring Captain Raynsford in a temporary grave with one of the quartermaster sergeant's wooden crosses at the head. By a strange coincidence, Raynsford's permanent grave in the St Manvieu War Cemetery is at almost the same spot as his temporary burial place.

The 2NY's baptism of fire took place across open cornfields. The 1NY's first attack took them through the notorious *Bocage*, a region of tiny fields, each one hedged about like a ready-made fortress, with hedges so high and thick that no tank commander could see over them or through them. They were set on banks 2ft or 3ft high, causing the tank to climb up and show its thinly plated underbelly to any marksmen beyond the hedge. The Germans frequently used the *Panzerfaust*, a hand-held, one-shot, throw-away bomb projector fired by a single infantryman and, at 50 yards, quite powerful enough to disable the tank. Some of the fields were not much larger than a tennis court and few were large enough for a full-scale football match. These fields could be death traps even for tanks and infantry working together in close liaison. Armoured brigade regiments like 1NY, 144 RAC and 148 RAC were farmed out to infantry formations as needed in Normandy. So the tank crews of C Squadron, 1NY had never met the Green Howards of the 50th Infantry Division, with whom they were to work on 30 June, as they aimed to secure a dozen or so of the tiny fields and reach the farm of La Taille.

Lieutenant Tony Faulkner encountered the first problem on the start line of the planned attack, finding only a few infantrymen waiting there. They had been in constant action over the D-Day beaches, where their CSM Stan Hollis gained the Victoria Cross, and through the *Bocage* without respite in some of the worst close combat fighting of the war; the men were exhausted. One encounter had been earned. It was obvious that this would be an unsupported tank probe. Jock Troup was one of the subsequent casualties:

We crashed through the first hedge, I was firing machine-gun bursts up and down the hedgerows. Then the tank stopped. Not a word from anyone. I hadn't seen a gun flash but I fired off an H.E. shot anyway. Had we been hit? There was a smell of acrid smoke and red hot metal. We had been told we had only seven seconds to get out if the tank went up. My power traverse wasn't working. I made a scramble for the turret exit – where was Frank Hickson, my commander? I rolled over the side of the tank. My clothes were burnt. I waved to some stretcher bearers carrying someone away. They waved back. Then I saw they were going in the opposite direction: Germans! Face, hands, feet now very sore. Then I saw Frank lying on his back. I shouted 'Frank are you OK?' I got beside him. His eyes were closed and his life gurgled away. How did he get there? What hit him? My theory is we took two 88 armour-piercing shots. And the shock stopped me thinking/feeling. The first shot must have hit the front and killed the drivers. The second into the turret. Then a darkened face popped out of a hole and said 'who goes there?' I could only say 'Tank'. The infantryman crawled out of his hole and began putting a first aid dressing on my hands.

Jock was evacuated by air to Gloucester and spent three weeks in a burns unit. He learned later that a Panther tank had hidden in the hedges while the Shermans went by. Four NY tanks were burned out but Trooper Harry Graham knocked out two Panthers, the first such success for 1NY, although the area of La Taille farm remained a no-man's-land. Later, Captain Bill Fox went out to check on the lost tanks. He knew that Stan Hicken's friend Bill Rawlins had been killed and asked if Stan would like to drive the jeep. To their surprise, near Jock Troup's tank the Germans had buried the NY dead with military honours, a cross at the head of each grave. One of the Germans had scrawled in charcoal on Bill Rawlins' tank a German phrase meaning simply 'You didn't have a chance'.

The Yeomanry lads were still only learning the full horror of fighting in the Sherman tank, to which the Germans had given the name of the 'Tommy Cooker' because of its

Lieutenant Brown (1NY) explains day's orders to tank commanders Sergeant Upstone, Corporals Sumner and Dwight. *(IWM B9798)*

tendency to explode into fire, especially if hit in the engine with its 150 gallons of high-octane fuel. The crew might be lucky to have as much as the seven seconds that Jock Troup had heard mentioned. A tank could burn for hours, melting the armoured steel and glowing a golden orange like a monstrous incandescent electric bulb. Trooper Les 'Spud'Taylor never forgot the day when, merely inquisitive, he had first peered inside a knocked-out tank near the beaches:

> The AP shot had penetrated the left side of the turret. I climbed up to have a look in the turret.The stench was indescribable. I saw the loader-operator, his hands frozen in the act of feeding a belt of ammo into his machine-gun, his head resting sideways on his arm.The appalling thing was, the body was as black as coal from an advanced state of decay.The gunner was just a shapeless mass of decomposition on the turret floor. But the most horrific sight of all was the crew commander.The projectile on entry had decapitated the poor man. His body lay on the floor but the head, as if on display, rested upside down on a ledge, the lower jaw shot away. I was overcome by nausea.

The 2NY's travail around Cheux was not at an end and the Yeomen were to learn salutary lessons. On the instructions of 4th Armoured Brigade of 11th Armoured Division, two squadrons were sent forward in the late evening and night of 29/30 June to support infantry thought to have been isolated in the *Bocage*. They had no night sights or experience of night fighting. They managed to penetrate the general area of tiny fields indicated and on the way they were shot at more than once by British units on their flanks as their Cromwell tanks were not yet familiar to other units. In the confusion they were virtually surrounded and attacked by heavier German tanks as well as infantry. Requests to brigade for permission to retire were refused. By the roll call next morning more than half a squadron was 'missing' and that meant fifty personnel, including the squadron leader, Major Bobby Peel, second-in-command Captain Haig Edgar and three lieutenants. A German prisoner taken in the confusion stated that the enemy were able to sight their guns on the exhaust backfires and gun flashes of the Cromwell guns, whereas the lesser flashes of the German guns gave the Yeomen few targets to aim at with their virtually blind gun telescopes. It was not the last time that the troopers might have regretted being the recce unit of the 'Charging Bull' division.[2]

By Normandy standards the NY losses were minor incidents, while another Yeomanry regiment, 4th County of London (4CLY), suffered a much more severe blow. It advanced into the path of the German army's elite Tiger tank company commanded by leading 'tank ace' Major Michael Wittmann, veteran of Russia and the Balkans. The 4CLY were now to bear the brunt of the British Army's learning experience and planning failures. Perhaps the pivotal town on the British front next in importance to Caen was Villers-Bocage, and the 7th Armoured Division had driven well ahead in an attempt to capture this objective. Almost as though on an exercise, the leading armour of the division had reached their point on the map and halted ready for future dispositions. Just then Wittmann in his tank, reconnoitring ahead as was his wont, came round a bend in the road and, with practised precision ran his single Tiger past the waiting British tanks, his great 88mm gun knocking out more than twenty vehicles; his massive front plating impervious to any 4CLY guns, even had there been opportunity for the gunners to respond. Wittmann then drove into Villers-Bocage and a battle ensued. Wittmann's own tank was temporarily knocked out, but he survived for another Yeomanry regiment to exact vengeance later on. The drive to take Villers-Bocage withered away for the time being, and 4CLY were later amalgamated with 3CLY to continue fighting in Normandy. Meanwhile, as General Montomery's first-day intentions lengthened into a month, Caen still remained an impediment to the British advance.

By D-Day +30 1NY had endured weeks of 'fire brigade' activity, moving from one counterattack position to another to reinforce the infantry. Now the Northants troopers, advancing with the King's Shropshire Light Infantry and the Royal Ulster Rifles through Lebissey Woods, became spectators at a unique air display. Over their head thundered wave after wave of heavy bombers, not just dozens but hundreds in strict formation. A curtain of anti-aircraft fire rose up around Caen 2 miles away. As bombs began to drop the curtain diminished, sagged and disappeared. Bombs continued to drop. Tanks shuddered and bounced on their springs from the effects of the blasts; deafened Yeomen and infantrymen watched, waved, cheered. Surely nobody could survive such an onslaught? (Sadly thousands of French civilians failed to survive. Most of the German troops had quietly retreated.)

Arriving on the heights overlooking the Orne River outside Caen, a strange thing happened. C Squadron was ordered to shoot at a distant factory at Colombelles, so nineteen tanks lined up and fired at high chimneys, suspected of being observation points. Gunner Ron West obeyed when his commander ordered 'Cease fire!', but knowing that there was no problem with his gun, Ron queried the order. The sergeant replied, 'I don't believe in this war business. I am declaring peace!' and promptly fainted. The perplexed trooper squeezed out of the turret past the limp commander. At that moment RSM Jelley and Captain Fox with two lorries were coming along the line of tanks, throwing replacement ammunition up to loaders. They immediately called the medical half-track and the sergeant was whisked away down the evacuation route to be attended by psychiatrists. The attitude towards genuine cases of battle shock was much more enlightened than in the 'shot at dawn' days of earlier wars.

With their ears still ringing from the bomber raid and the intense barrage fired at the factory, 3 Baker, Stan Hicken's tank commanded by former school teacher Corporal Ken Snowdon, was ordered to lead 3 Troop down the main road into Caen as night fell, on an exploratory mission. As Stan followed the main road from the coast into Caen the tarmac disappeared at the point where the streets should have started. Instead there was a vast moonscape of mountainous rubble and vast gorges in the earth – the visiting card of the RAF. Stan began to drive carefully over what might have been a tank-proving ground at Bovington camp:

> There were two of our reconnaissance tanks in flames on the left that had tried to travel that way before us. We plodded on and suddenly descended into a huge bomb crater or series of craters. The steep angle that we went down caused a Sten gun to slip off the top of the wireless and hit the operator, Tommy Tucker, on the head. Ken Snowdon managed to climb up the crater side to see what was happening and liaise with [Lieutenant] Bobby McColl and the Ulsters' officer. Our gunner, Ken Tout, stood on the tank turret but he couldn't see over the edge of the crater. The order came 'Pull back'. As we had come down on a fairly straight line I decided to rev up as much as I could and reverse straight out, not veering to left or right or we would have rolled over. Next morning Hank Bevan came along to us and said, 'Congratulations, you got the first tank into Caen! You will be able to tell your grandchildren that.' 20 year old Tommy replied 'I haven't got any grandchildren, sir.' To which the Major responded 'You carry on the way you do and you'll have 500'. Full marks to Hank.

NY Recce Sergeant Kenny Jack MM had managed to climb, scramble and stumble over the rubble, partly on foot and partly on knees, and reported back confirming 3 Baker's verdict that there was no passage for vehicles, not even for bulldozers, into the centre of Caen. This would have fatal consequences on 2NY, 2nd Fife and Forfar Yeomanry, 4CLY and many others. Unable to progress through Caen, British armour would now have to swing north and east about, and then turn west across the wide level Caen plain under the shadow of the next obstacle on the road to Paris, the long gentle Bourguebus Ridge, perhaps the most deceiving feature in Normandy when compared to steep, sharp hills like Mont Pincon. The straight main road to Falaise rose gradually up the low ridge with no ominous sign of impending disaster. But from any point on the ridge the defender could look down on all that moved below. Lethal German 88mm and improved 75mm guns dominated the scene across which massed, inadequately armoured British and Canadian forces must move.

In 18 July Montgomery launched those forces in Operation Goodwood, later named 'the Death Ride of the armoured divisions'. The Scottish Yeomen of the F&F, with the 23rd Hussars and 2RTR formed the spearhead and suffered huge casualties. The high commanders had failed to provide sufficient infantry 'up front' to assist the tanks in locations where only infantry could make progress. The 2NY with adequate infantry of the Herefords and Monmouths cleared two villages with minimal casualties, but the infantry could not keep up with the tanks. The 2NY also entered the death ride, as did the Guards and the 7th Armoured Division (Desert Rats), yet more tanks beneath the muzzles of the enemy guns. It was the 'Charge of the Light Brigade' on a much vaster scale. Typical of the front units, 2NY lost forty-seven out of sixty-two tanks but remarkably, within two days, had been brought back up to strength by replacement tanks and reinforcement crews. Trooper W.R. 'Bill' Moseley saw what had happened to the first attacks as 2NY, moving on from its first successful Goodwood action in Cuverville and Demouville, caught up with the spearhead:

What a sight met our eyes: our periscopes revealed that the whole area was strewn with the smoke-blackened carcases of the 29th Brigade's Sherman tanks … some with their turrets blown off; others still 'brewing' with gouts of orange flame shooting skywards from hatches as ammunition exploded; dead bodies hanging from escape hatches at grotesque angles: dismounted crews trying to rescue wounded comrades; others attempting to mend broken tracks; all amid the swirling black smoke from burning fuel. As the flashes of mortar bombs raining down lit up the smoke it was a scene from Dante's INFERNO bought to life.[3]

Moseley's spectator amazement did not last long before his own squadron was engulfed in anti-tank fire. The flat area was dominated by a high railway embankment, on one side of which tanks were relatively safe but hampered as to advance. The other side was the killing ground. Moseley's commander, Dougie, ordered the tank to follow others through a railway arch:

No sooner had we emerged than we were under heavy fire from an orchard. These were ANGRY MEN and they were firing at US. Dougie ordered me to plaster the orchard with HE. But the tank SHUDDERED to a stop. Engine dead. Dougie yelled 'Bale out!' I took a flying leap out and landed among the others who were flat on their faces. Our turret belched fire. We made a dash for Sgt Tite's tank. I perched on the track guard. Next thing I knew – a frightening THUD and a shower of sparks engulfed my feet. An AP shot had ploughed through the armour plate, shattering the idler wheel, missing the co-driver and my feet by inches. We were both burned by the heat as the shot sheared through metal. Another thud and the cry 'Bale out!' And like 'bats out of hell' we were running for cover as MG bullets zipped around us, kicking up the dust. We were sniped and mortared all the way.

Amid it all there was a moment of black humour. As they trudged back beyond the embankment a commander from a non-Yeomanry unit saw their badges and shouted, 'What up, mates? Lost your effing horses?' Driver Albert drew his pistol, aimed it at the commander, shouting, 'Cheeky bastard, I'll effing do you!', before Dougie and Bill wrestled Albert's pistol from him. Fitter Sergeant Sid Jones, following the tanks in his half-track, later assumed that the German commander had coolly watched fourteen tanks of the squadron pass through the railway arch and then, seeing Sid's half-track at the tail, calculated that it was a complete unit and opened fire to eliminate most of the tanks. Sid had watched the first tank pass through the arch:

> It halted, waited a while. There were no shots at us or by us. The remainder of B squadron then moved through, near Soliers on the Bray road. My carrier had moved 50 yards out of the arch when all hell broke loose. I then gave my driver orders to turn round and make for the safe side of the embankment. We fitters then dismounted and went to see to the wounded. One had facial injuries, his top lip was gone and he was bleeding profusely, his clothing and hair soaked with blood. We did not know what to do to stop it. We put masses of shell dressing over his face but the floor of the half-track was covered with blood. We took a load of wounded back to the field ambulances. Later we found it was the major with his face bleeding, so blooded that we did not recognise him or see his rank badges. Going back we found one tank apparently serviceable. There was a body lying on the engine cover. It had been decapitated. We identified it as Trooper Niblock. We put the headless body in a blanket and buried him in the soft earth of the embankment.

Approximately half of the tanks involved in Operation Goodwood were knocked out. Bill Moseley described some of those as 'burning an orange colour through the night'. Some of the tanks could be recovered, but the enemy still sat up along most of the slopes of the Bourguebus Ridge in spite of Montgomery's premature claim that a complete breakthrough towards Falaise had been achieved. A Yeomanry troop of 4CLY, led by Lieutenant John Cloudsley-Thompson, achieved the farthest thrust forward across the main Caen-Falaise road. However, a Canadian artillery barrage was due to fall on them and so they were withdrawn. As they did so, fellow tank soldiers were amazed to see Firefly gunner Bob Moore hit and destroy an enemy tank at the incredible range for a tank gun of 2,300 yards, the Firefly gun proving better than the feared Tiger's 88mm. On 20 July a massive storm and subsequent floods brought Operation Goodwood to an end.

The problem of the Bourguebus Ridge was handed to a Canadian, Lieutenant General Guy Simonds. The British 51st Highland Division and the 33rd Armoured Brigade were put under the orders of his Canadian corps, which had suffered heavy losses in the earlier fighting. Having studied the failures of Goodwood, Simonds made some original decisions: he would attack by night, he would drive straight through the German defences with armoured columns and he would put infantry well up with the armour by producing armoured infantry carriers. The lead divisional commander of Goodwood, Major General Roberts, had wanted to do something similar but higher authority vetoed the idea. And there were no carriers available in early August 1944, although the tank founders had been experimenting with armoured carriers in 1917.

Simonds simply borrowed seventy-six self-propelled guns from the Americans and, within five days, had the guns taken out, the gaps filled in and thus produced carriers able to carry a section of infantry in each. The carriers soon obtained the name of Kangaroos. The entire operation was to be called 'Totalize'.

What that meant to Ray Ager and his mates on Captain Tom Boardman's tank of A Squadron, 1NY, was that they were told to make themselves scarce, go to the NAAFI canteen which had appeared near them and not come back until sent for. Strange signallers took over the tank. On return Ray and the others found all kinds of new gadgets fitted into the tank, in order to help Tom Boardman navigate in the dark across open country. There would be seven armoured columns, the tanks lined up in rows of four, the lead infantry Kangaroos a few rows back behind the tanks and minesweeping 'Crabs'. The three British tank colonels were allowed to form their columns as they considered fit: Lieutenant Colonel Doug Forster placed Tom Boardman ahead as a lead navigator with Captain Ken Todd as second navigator; in 144 RAC the colonel chose to lead with three light 'Honey' tanks; while the four Canadian columns also had slightly different formations.

At 11 p.m. on 7 August another massed RAF raid took place, aiming to seal off the flanks of the Night March. Although their targets were only 800 yards from the left files of 1NY, not a bomb fell on the tanks in a magnificent display of air navigation and bomb aiming. At 11.30 p.m. the amour rolled away with orders not to stop but

Crew loading shells on to Sergeant Ginns' 1NY Sherman Firefly before the 'Night March', 7 August 1944. *(IWM B8793)*

'bash on'. Drivers followed the red tail lights of the tanks in front of them. Coloured shells were fired overhead in the general direction of the objective 5 miles away. There was inevitably some chaos and confusion in a style of attack for which training in the UK had not been provided, and the planned rehearsals required by Simonds had been cut short by an impatient Montgomery. Lieutenant A.R. Burn, commanding a Lothian and Border Yeomanry 'Crab', was astonished to see the four vehicles ahead of him in thick mist 'divide themselves conveniently driving to the four winds, N.S.E. and W., and were never seen again', leaving Burn with the problem of finding another red tail light to follow. Just behind Boardman and Todd, Trooper Derek Roberts heard some of the problems in his earphones:

> Suddenly radio silence was shattered. It was a voice of some authority trying to contact the two front tanks. He failed to make contact and turned his attention to us, 4 Charlie. Our [sergeant] Dick Moralee answered immediately 'No, sir, we haven't seen their lights for some time'. There was so much mist, smoke and dust. There was a moment's silence. Then the voice said 'Send up a flair'. I sorted the pistol and cartridge and Dick fired it off. After a time came the now very irate voice, 'Come on, man. Put a move on. Fire that flare'. Dick replied 'I sent one up, sir'. The voice somewhat mollified, 'Then send up another. Send up a white' – there being green and red all over the sky. I found a white and Dick fired. The voice obviously had his mike switched on for we heard 'What's the bloody man doing ... no, can't see it ... where? Oh, yes, over THERE!' At which point Capt Boardman's voice cut in. He himself had fired off all his Very lights and had walked back to Capt Todd's tank to get another supply. All in the night blinded by a million flashes, somewhere in a Normandy potato field.

The NY column 'bashed on' and reached the objective before 3 a.m. on 8 August. The 144 RAC had less luck: their three lighter, smaller navigator tanks all disappeared, one of them literally below ground level, in bomb craters, and Lieutenant Colonel Jolly had to come forward himself to navigate. At the NY objective Lieutenant Colonel Hopwood of the Black Watch took over from his NY colleague and, with sixty tank guns giving covering fire, sent his Kangaroos right up to the cottages being defended by the Germans. In a very brief period, and with a tenth of the normally calculated casualties, the Black Watch had occupied the vital high village of Saint-Aignan-de-Cramesnil. The NY tanks, like those of the other columns, moved forward of the village and found themselves hides from which to repel counterattacks. The seven columns had smashed through a fresh, well-trained, full-strength German division two days after its arrival.

However, the former defenders, the elite 12th SS Panzers *Hitlerjugend* ('Hitler Youth'), who had been ordered to Mortain in an attempt to cut off the now rapidly advancing Americans, were still lurking just beyond Saint-Aignan. Their commander, Kurt Meyer, also known as 'Panzermeyer', ordered an immediate counterattack. He had available five of the very few Tigers left in service at this time and, rather precipitately, he ordered Michael Wittmann to advance across the open cornfields before the main counterattack by the 12th SS Panzers could get moving. The objective was 'to regain the vital heights around Saint-Aignan', a suicidal venture consistent with the German doctrine of immediate counterattack.

A 30-ton Sherman Firefly, here at St Aignan, which later knocked out three 50-ton German Tigers on this skyline, 8 August 1944. *(1994 reconstruction by Old Coaches, St Malo, NYA)*

On the west of the Caen-Falaise road near Gaumesnil, Major Radley-Walters' Sherbrooke Fusiliers, in their Sherman tanks, had already been firing at lesser fry. Wittmann's Tigers turned their guns in that direction. On the east of the road at Saint-Aignan, Sergeant Gordon of A Squadron, 1NY, in his Firefly, spotted the Tigers and reported back. Captain Boardman ordered Gordon to hold fire and brought three 75mm Shermans into line with the Firefly. He ordered the smaller-gunned Shermans to 'pepper' the Tigers and force the commanders to duck down into turrets, before Gunner Joe Ekins then fired successive 17-pounder shots which knocked out three Tigers. The Sherbrookes firing from the other flank accounted for the rear Tiger. Wittmann died in the battle and, in a way, the action at Villers-Bocage was avenged.

In the early 1980s Jean-Claude Pallud located Wittmann's 1944 grave, and erstwhile NY Trooper Les 'Spud' Taylor published a full review in *After the Battle*. Since then much debate has centred on the theme 'Who killed Wittmann?' However, it misses an essential point. Even with Wittmann's Tigers eliminated, the 12th SS Panzers had been ordered to retake the heights, and had they done so the full array of Canadian armour would still have been exposed to superior German guns. Panzermeyer sent battle group KG Waldmuller, a combined arms formation which could be assembled immediately with whatever type of force was needed and available, to capture Saint-Aignan. It was this type of mobilisation for a specific task which the Germans had perfected but the British had not yet implemented to any considerable extent.

As the KG moved off from the area around Robertmesnil farm, showers of mortar bombs rained down on the NY and Black Watch positions. 'Shower' is no exaggeration, for a German barrage could consist of numbers of the *Nebelwerfer* bomb projectors, each firing at least six bombs at once, setting up a huge concert of screaming sirens as the infamous and aptly named 'Moaning Minnies' descended vertically on the foe. Tank commanders closed down and infantry ducked low in slit trenches. At this initial point a voice spoke on the wireless, audible to all crews:

'Hullo, Baker. Hullo, Baker. Medics to Big Sunray. Medics to Big Sunray. Baker, over.'

It was someone on Big Sunray's tank calling to the second-in-command for aid, and Big Sunray was the colonel, Doug Forster, himself. This was a blast of reality for the listening crews, triumphant from the Night March. A minute into battle and the colonel had been wounded, or worse. Within seconds the wireless came alive again, this time B Squadron leader's operator calling for immediate aid to Major the Hon. Peter Brassey, also a shrapnel victim. 'Starting from the top and working down?' somebody in Stan Hicken's tank commented. Major Philip Wykeham would take over command, but the colonel had always seemed invincible, imperturbable, immovable.

Then movements in the corn, golden to harvest, indicated that the fanatical but eminently skilful *Hitlerjugend* were on their way, determined to recapture Saint-Aignan. Between the village and Robertmesnil farm there appeared on the map and aerial photographs to be a country lane running as a kind of ride through thick woods. The SS Panzer Corps HQ had been located at Robertmesnil and the German troops knew very well that the innocent country lane was in fact a narrow but extremely deep defile, *Le Petit Ravin*. Many of the German Mk IV tanks crawled unseen along this 'gulley'. The German infantry were unfortunate in the weather, a blazing hot day, and as the NY machine-gun fire tore through the cornfields the ripe corn caught fire. The *Jugend* had three choices: rush forward exposed, retreat, or stand and be grilled or asphyxiated. Many rushed forward, but not far.

Trooper Joe Crittenden spotted another Tiger tank, the last, and halted it at long range. Stan Hicken and Rex Jackson, low down in their driver's compartment on the lip of the gulley, discerned the cautious movement of a tank shape through the trees. The maze of greenery in which 3 Baker was hiding made the tank invisible to Corporal Ken Snowdon and the gunner. Stan and Rex 'talked' the gun around to the correct position and Snowdon ordered 'Fire', despatching the enemy tank with two well-aimed shots. Gunner Ernie Wellbelove, the smallest man in the squadron, saw three enemy tanks running across a field and shot two of them, while the third raced behind a large haystack. Ernie continued to fire his 17-pounder through the haystack; a burst of flame and cloud of back smoke told of his third success. Sadly, within minutes, another Mk IV had crawled along the gulley and emerged from behind to knock out Ernie's tank, killing the popular lad instantaneously. Nevertheless, Panzermeyer's attempt to recapture the crucial village of Saint-Aignan had been beaten off.

Large-scale operations demanded only a small proportion of the days after D-Day. Most days were minor actions, maintenance or frustration with military systems. Sergeant Kenny Jack MM recalled a moment at Demouville where the men were being

The 2NY Cromwells greeted by French civilians during liberation of Flers, Normandy, August 1944. *(IWM B9329)*

eaten alive by mosquitoes. They were in a counterattack position in their light tank, hidden in trees on a flat plain with large signs declaring 'DUST MEANS DEATH':

> We were to keep look-out east but definitely not to be seen! We made ourselves comfortable, had something to eat, looked east and were invisible. Any movement brought shelling down instantly. Then one of the crew said 'What the hell is this?' Coming up was a staff car, flags waving, a general studying his map and flourishing his cane in the direction of any suspected Jerry OP [observation post]. At least half a dozen vehicles with him raising dust. Then off they went just as fast. Down came the inevitable mortar 'stonk'. Crash! Bang! Crash! I knew something was wrong. Young Tony Martin who was out of the tank for natural purposes had a bad shrapnel wound in the thigh. I had better not repeat the words I said about the general.

Corporal Doug Gardner was also peeved about petty authorities. The summer of 1944 brought much rain to Normandy and Doug's Firefly wireless set was being affected by leaking water. In the Firefly, to accommodate the larger gun, the wireless was fixed into an extra armoured box at the rear of the turret:

> I had continual trouble with rain leaking into the tray beneath the set and rendering it useless. So I thought 'if we can't stop the water getting in, then let's drain it out'. We bored six holes in the bottom of the box and this did the trick. Then we had a routine inspection of the tank by Corps engineers. On seeing the holes we had drilled, the Officer gave me a real b★★★★★ dressing down – it was against regulations – so he had his chaps weld up the holes. I was concerned about the set packing up when you were in action. Then … a few days later an Engineers unit came round to implement a SPECIAL War Office modification to the Firefly – yes, you've guessed it – it was to drill six holes in the wireless box to let the water drain out!!!

Before the Normandy campaign ended 2NY had one more moment of battle trauma to endure, followed by an even more devastating attack on them by High Command. After the grim suffering on the open plain beyond Caen, 2NY, like the rest of the 'Charging Bull' units, had been reinforced. They now found that they had advanced once again into *Bocage* country around Flers as a part of Operation Bluecoat. General Montgomery had originally intended a large encirclement to the River Seine along the route followed by 1NY, but now mounted Bluecoat to hold German forces in the Flers area whilst the Canadian/Polish thrust linked up with American General Patton's troops in a shorter encirclement.

In the earlier *Bocage* battles there had always been a sense knowing where the enemy was located, often to within yards. One survivor remembered Germans throwing a snake over a hedge at his position, to which he replied by returning the snake. So close! Now nobody knew quite where the enemy might be over wider distances of confused terrain. Fitter Sid Jones with his half-track was repairing a Cromwell tank behind the main squadron when a great noise of complaining engines in the trees behind him, from which 2NY were advancing, convinced him that it was a Tiger tank. Sid and his mates dived into a ditch and prepared to fight Tigers with pistols and puny Sten guns. In fact, not one but two Tigers rumbled past without bothering them or shooting up their vehicle, no doubt as disorientated as Sid's crew were.

There were a few brief moments of glory during the confused advance. Fortified villages in the area of Caen and Cheux had been mainly devoid of civilians, but in Flers civilians came out in thousands and even hindered the progress of the 2NY tanks as the crews waved back, enjoying the rare moment. It was then back to reality as Bill Moseley so vividly noted:

> We had been told by a French civilian that the Jerries had retreated. My eyes glued to the gun telescope we had just breasted a rise … T-junction … cottage … range 200 yards – I saw an 88mm gun pointing straight at us … adrenaline pumped … X-wires on target amid a babble of voices … 'Bloody 88' … 'Brass him up, Ken' [to the hull gunner] … 'Get him, Mose! Driver, reverse! Fire!' and my foot stabbed the firing button – WOOMP – gun flash, recoil, shell exploding – and as the tank reverses over the crest, no return fire, and Ron, with field glasses 'You got him, Mose … Poor buggers didn't stand a chance … let's go take a look … carefully.'

Even in the heat of battle common humanity prevailed at times. Moseley was surprised to see a French farmer walking a horse in a field in the midst of battle. The farmer signalled that the horse had been horribly wounded by shellfire and needed to be put down:

> Dickie tried to shoot it with bullets from his .38 pistol but the bullets only bounced off the skull of the poor animal which was frantic, with the farmer hanging on to the bridle for dear life. The only way we could end the beast's agony was with a burst of Sten gun into the heart. The farmer thanked us and scarpered, not looking too sad and maybe thinking of freshly butchered horse steaks on the morrow.

Hard fighting and humane acts, however, would not save the Second Line. As the Normandy campaign drew to a close the colonel called the regiment together to pass on the bad news: they were to be disbanded, immediately, on the spot, hand over their beloved tanks to a new mob. The 2NY now paid the final price for lack of seniority. Units normally going into battle for the first time need some time to adjust and to acquire the very specific attitudes and reactions that only live fire against the enemy can generate. Good sense might suggest that if fresh troops were available they could be used as reinforcements to merge into a now battle-experienced and toughened unit. But the arriving 15th/19th Hussars were a more senior regiment, and that was the vital criterion. On the night of 17/18 August the Hussars arrived to take over 2NY's tanks.

Bill Moseley, Captain Sandy Saunders and fifty others were relieved to know that they were going as reinforcements to their First Line, where they knew many people and shared a common Yeomanry culture. Reg Spittles was not sure as to what he might expect when, with his entire troop and three others, he was transferred to 1RTR. When he joined up the NY had been an armoured car unit of the RTC, now the RTR, but war might have changed things since then. Other men that transferred to other Hussars regiments were not sure if there would be a difference between Yeomanry traditions and the regular cavalry, although the difference between regulars, TA soldiers and more recent conscripts had now, to a large extent, been eliminated. Two months of battle had cost 2NY total casualties of thirty-two officers and 196 ORs. The total tank crew strength of the three 2NY fighting squadrons in action was only 273 and thus required constant reinforcement.

Sandy Saunders and the other 2NY men joining the First Line were on the move again without pause. Driving towards the Seine alongside the 51st Highland Division, 1NY found itself, on more than one occasion, ordered to halt in order to keep formation with units on either side. One such enforced halt on the road to Lisieux proved to be the nemesis of revered SSM Sid Turton. With enemy on three sides, the squadron waited in a farmer's field. Occasional deliveries of 'Moaning Minnies' caused troopers to dive inside or underneath tanks for cover. During one such dive the SSM went first under the tank, followed by Sergeant Len Wright, just back from hospital, and Trooper Bruce Dickson. By some miracle a bomb bounced under the tank without exploding, rolled over Len and Bruce and exploded against the SSM. Len Wright went back to hospital again but Bruce emerged physically unharmed, and because he soldiered on he did not receive any treatment for shock and would suffer nightmares for years afterwards, an experience of so many who did not benefit from the immediate psychiatric treatment provided for those with more visible effects of battle shock.

Sid Turton was buried immediately while the farmer's family brought armfuls of flowers to adorn the grave. A problem then arose for Acting Major Bill Fox with Hank Bevan now at regimental HQ. The SSM had been commanding a captain's tank and the only other officers surviving were Lieutenants Faulkner and McColl, who were needed to command leading troops. Lance corporals were already commanding a number of tanks and Bill Fox now called one of them, the author, to command the spare captain's tank. This state of affairs lasted for about two weeks until the colonel and others returned from hospital, together with more postings from the now disbanded 2NY. It was a quiet complaint among tank crews that whilst in the RAF every crew member had to be at least a sergeant, on the ground unpaid lance corporals had to command tanks leading attacks, with many quickly becoming casualties.

The 1NY's travelogue continued with the siege of the port and naval base at Le Havre. The regiment's sixty tanks lined up and, at the colonel's command on 'A' set: 'All stations Able … stand by to fire … five rounds gunfire … NOW!', all tanks fired a total of sixty rounds each indirectly (highly elevated guns) at enemy defensive targets previously registered by the colonel and Major Bevan. Then the attack led up the hill to the huge naval barracks where one lonely shot came from a huge naval 380mm gun, which fortunately could not depress enough to fire down the hill.[4] A few shots from two of C Squadron's relatively puny 75mm guns caused doors to swing open, and over a thousand naval personnel marched out in good order behind a white flag.[5]

The war had now switched into Belgium and Holland. The ill-fated attempt to capture Arnhem by airborne attack had left the Allies with a problem, as the main Arnhem road stretched for almost 40 miles with the enemy still firmly ensconced along its length. There would now be the painful task of advancing outwards from both sides, liberating village after village as the Germans slowly and cleverly retreated, often ceding ground but always blowing up the next of the many bridges over rivers and canals.

German troops were still retreating from the Channel ports and their escape route was over the last bridge of the mighty River Maas. The 1NY was part of the week-long operation to reach and close off this vital bridge. At Loon-op-Zand, Corporal Ken Snowdon's tank in 3 Troop, C Squadron, often in the lead, was at last 'brewed up', although the crew escaped. In the chaos of battle Stan Hicken's co-driver Rex Jackson rescued a burning tank and was awarded the Military Medal. The last objective was the village of Raamsdonk overlooking the final vital Maas bridge.

The two-day battle in Raamsdonk was typical of many at the time, involving two squadrons of tanks and a battalion of Highland infantry, with the enemy resolutely defending fortified buildings along the village street. The Allies were attacking in much greater force than the defenders and, as in Raamsdonk, the objective was usually gained at the cost of, in military terms, relatively few tanks, which could be rapidly replaced, and a few memorial crosses planted along the route. NY tanks at last obtained the dominating view of the bridge and in the smoke-filled streets the firing had died down. As in the outskirts of Caen long before, Lieutenant Bobby McColl got out of his tank to confer with the infantry. A last German gunner fired off a few final few machine-gun bullets and the 19-year-old troop leader was killed instantaneously. Major Hank Bevan sat down to write yet another last letter to shocked parents at home.

Christmas seemed to be bringing a winter lull in fighting and a time to fraternise with happy Dutch civilians. Hitler, however, had other ideas, launching the so-called 'Battle of the Bulge' through the Ardennes in an effort to reach Antwerp and thus cut off the northern Allied armies from the forces to the south. The unexpected charge broke through thin American defences and, for a while, threatened to cause great havoc. The German generals themselves had doubts about the possibility of achieving Hitler's vision and, as British troops were rushed to aid the Americans, the attacks petered out. For men like the 1NY tank crews, the overriding memories were not so much of battle but of perishing cold to the body and danger to the tanks as they slithered up and down steep, forested, icy slopes for which no tank was designed. Captain Sandy Saunders thought it must have been '275 degrees below zero', although the actual 40 degrees below was bad enough:

It was COLD! It was bloody cold in the open air! It was even colder standing in the turret of a Sherman tank with the air being sucked in beside you to the engine intake, freezing your overalls while you sweated with fear. Added to this, 30 tons of Sherman weight did not prevent the tanks from skidding all over the icy roads. Bad, downright dangerous on the ski-type slopes. Even in villages. The tank in front of us, meaning to go straight on, was caught by a wrong camber in the road and slid off sideways down a steep side street and the driver could do nothing about it. If you caught your track on a kerb and broke it you had to get out and haul huge lengths of frozen metal to mend the thing. We could hardly be bothered about what the Germans might be aiming at us – arctic survival was our main purpose.

Sandy was later called by a Belgian civilian to examine a pile of more than thirty civilians, each of whom had been shot in the head and all of them dumped in a local cellar. A little while earlier NY tanks, with the Argyll and Sutherland Highlanders alongside, had come upon the notorious Kamp Vught where the Nazis had imprisoned Dutch and Belgian civilians, shooting many there in the grounds and exporting even more by rail to killing camps in Germany. The 20-year-old Yeomen were learning hard lessons about 'man's inhumanity to man'.

The next great barrier to cross was the River Rhine, after which the wide German plains would be open to the overwhelming armoured might of the Allies. Once again Yeomanry regiments proved their adaptability in battle, as the NY and ERY were now switched to driving the amphibious Buffalo, essentially a crude armoured steel box which floated and could carry a Bren gun carrier, an anti-tank gun or a section of infantry across the treacherous currents of the Rhine. Grousers (extensions) added to the track links enabled the tracks to propel the clumsy vehicles slowly through the water, though with limited steering ability. The Staffordshire Yeomen would once again use their waterproof Duplex-Drive swimming tanks to cross the river and give immediate gun support to the infantry. Other regiments continued their varied life, the Cheshires in the air-landing operation beyond the river and the Lothian and Borders sweeping minefields to reach the river, where the engineers would build a pontoon bridge.

As on 8 August 1944, so now in March 1945 NY troopers were dismayed before the battle started to hear that the colonel, Doug Forster DSO, had again been seriously

The 1NY amphibious Buffalo carrier loading up to cross the River Rhine, March 1945. *(Tank Museum/NYA)*

injured and would go back to England, never to return. Major the Lord George Scott came back from leave to find himself commanding the local crossing within hours. Major Hank Bevan MC and Captain Tom Boardman MC had gone forward to examine the *Bund*, the great anti-flood embankment which lined the river, marking routes and arranging for the engineers to blast gaps for the infantry.

One of the first awkward Buffaloes to move through the gap crashed and blocked it, with those following having to climb the seemingly vertical *Bund*, worse than any obstacle on the Bovington proving ground, pause at the top and then slide without control down into the rushing river in the dark. Once in the river the Buffalo had to be pointed diagonally downriver to avoid being swept too fast upriver and missing the marked landing beach. Remarkably, the Buffalo ferry service successfully landed two whole infantry divisions across the river and then assisted them over subsequent water obstacles. Not all crossings were without incident; for instance, Trooper Johnny Howell, just back from an appendicitis operation in England, had his vehicle swamped and found himself swimming for his life in rough, icy, oily, dark waters. Somehow Johnny survived, although all his portable personal belongings remain somewhere at the bottom of the Rhine.

With such an unwieldy, poorly controlled vehicle there were many alarms, crossing an unknown river in darkness exacerbated by explosion flashes which dazzled the eyes. Rex Jackson MM, now promoted and commanding a Buffalo driven by Mike Hunt, imagined the worst possible fate when, on their first return journey, the engine stalled in midstream:

Before we knew where we were the current had whipped us away, spinning round and round until, you might say, we didn't know our stern from our starboard. Mike got the engine going again but we were still spinning and it was impossible to see anything down there on the water, with mist and smoke adding to the darkness. Luckily the night before I had attended a commanders' briefing which included sight of an

This 1NY Buffalo was one of 79th Armoured Division's specially adapted tanks, or 'Funnies'.
(*NYA*)

extremely good scale model of the crossing area. There was a fixed crane on the home
side which was raised high near the track for follow-up loads. Now I could see it sil-
houetted against the night. We still had to get there. Mike managed to control the spin
and head to the bank. We TRIED to land. But the *Bund* here was lined with stone or
cement blocks on which the tracks would not grip. We slid back into the river which
whipped us downstream again. Eventually we were pushed into a lower bank, only to
find somebody pointing a machine gun at us, maybe thinking we were Germans on a
raid. We shouted the password at the top of our voices.

The Allied armies now pressed on into Germany from east and west. The NY troopers
were glad to be ordered to hand in their hated amphibians and travel to collect their
sleek Shermans again. Victory (VE) Day found them still dismounted in the city of
Zwolle and, as was happening to tired troops still in Holland, they were seized upon
by the joyful inhabitants and swept into a frenzied dance of delight which went on all
night. Next day there was more rejoicing and impromptu sports events. Later there was
a solemn memorial service in the great ancient church where the Roll of Honour was
read for the first time, mentioning so many remembered names of lost comrades.

As with those in the earlier Great War, credit must again be given to the 'Yeowomen'
of the First Aid Nursing Yeomanry (FANY). They excelled in various roles with many
of them also forming motor driver companies of the ATS, while others volunteered for
SOE, the perilous covert operations behind the enemy lines. Of those latter heroines

'Yeowomen' of the First Aid Nursing Yeomanry (FANY) in 1914. They later acquired motorised ambulances. *(PRVC/FANY, 2012)*

NY and 51st (Highland) Division veterans at the grave of NY's last fatal casualty, Corporal Hughie McGranahan, Hotton Cemetery, Ardennes. *(NYA)*

three won the supreme award of the George Cross, the non–combatant equivalent to the Victoria Cross. In all, fifty-four FANY members were killed in action in the two world wars.

Even in the very last days of April and May 1945 there had been fanatical resist-ance from some German units, and advancing soldiers had died right up to the last shots fired. The 2NY's Corporal Ken Jordan, now serving with the 8th Hussars, saw his troop leader, Lieutenant Wally Ryde, die even as the firing ended. Ken, later to become a minister of religion, helped his comrades carry the lieutenant's body into the local church and lay it before the altar, for they now had time to mourn before arranging a temporary burial. Seeing a garden nearby filled with beautiful flowers, Ken went rather hesitantly to the German *hausfrau* and asked permission to pick some flowers to place around the body. The woman immediately agreed and offered to join them for, she said, she herself had lost three sons on the Eastern Front. She would never get to mourn them at their remote, unknown graves, so she would join the British lads and mourn the lieutenant as one of her own.[6]

CHAPTER TEN

HANDS OFF THE TA!
(1947–2011)

V E Day did not signal immediate dissolution of the Yeomanry regiments and the Northants lads found themselves doing police and riot duty in the civil chaos that was Germany in the summer of 1945.

Stationed at the Hermann Goering steelworks, the NY had to preserve order among tens of thousands of slave labourers, all suddenly released but with no social organisation, material provisions, ability to travel or, in many cases, a surviving homeland to which they might return. There were also German ex-servicemen who had evaded prisoner-of-war camps and a German civilian population threatened by many persecuted victims of the Nazis now seeking vengeance. When order had been gradually restored the Yeomen were switched to commandeering vehicles in order to ensure delivery of basic supplies, and also undertaking lumberjack work as part of the reparations programme, with wood, machine tools, industrial blueprints and other items being shipped back to Britain.

In the autumn of 1946 the Yeomanry regiments were 'mothballed', or put into 'suspended animation', with the last Territorial soldiers demobilised and later as reinforcements posted to regular units. In the arcane military system Lieutenant Colonel the Lord George Scott closed down the Northamptonshire Yeomanry and the very next year the same Lord George re-formed the Northamptonshire Yeomanry as a unit of the re-established Territorial Army. The same thing was happening across the spectrum of county Yeomanry regiments as they were adapted into the varied roles which had become typical of the Yeomanry: several regiments became permanent field artillery units and some heavy artillery; the 3rd/4th County of London, the Wiltshires, and others drew tanks and served as armoured regiments; the Fife and Forfar were equipped with armoured cars; the Worcesters became anti-tank artillery; the Scottish Horse re-formed as the divisional RAC regiment of the Highland infantry division; and the North Somersets joined the airborne division. Perhaps few of them suspected that by the 1950s there would be further changes in their roles, reductions in size and amalgamations. Eventually, proud county regiments, many of whom had provided more than one regiment during the recent war, would find themselves diminished into ever smaller units with even more varied functions and regional amalgamations. By the twenty-first century the Northampton Drill Hall, where Sergeant Reg King had marked out bed spaces in 1939, would be home to the Royal Electrical and Mechanical Engineers (REME) Territorials.[1]

Virtually from the moment victory was declared there was hostility between the Western Allies and the USSR, and this was to escalate into the Cold War. It was essential, therefore, to maintain a full-size Territorial Army, available and ready for foreign service if needed. But for some time the normal peacetime status of the Yeomanry was affected by the new type of conscripted 'National Service' soldiers, and also by recall of reserves when the Cold War appeared to be reaching a 'Hot' state. John Bishop was called up for National Service and posted to the regular King's Dragoon Guards. He was then informed that the length of his service had been extended but that he could serve half of the time with the Territorials. He moved to the NY and continued to serve with them after the end of his National Service period.[2]

The 1NY's Doug Gardner had accepted his civilian suit after the war, gone home and hoped that the War Office had forgotten him forever, although theoretically all demobbed soldiers moved on to a Reserve List. He was disillusioned when it was decided to recall battle-experienced men for a fifteen-day refresher course. Recalled men, like Doug, were not amused:

> They made us run like chaff before the wind, and when kindly instructors tried to show us how to present arms, we carried on like Baboons with greased hands. Astonished Commanding Officers of suddenly inflated regiments had the duty of making welcome a roaring bunch of ageing civilians who, not without cause, prided themselves that they knew every trick worth while in the British Army. Many of us now held responsible positions in civilian life and/or were building up successful businesses. And a brief fortnight back with the boys was the purest tomfoolery. Fortunately the Russians did not attack.[3]

Territorial camps went ahead much as after the Boer War and Great War. In 1952 the NY went to camp at Lulworth ranges, under RSM A. England. George Jelley was still among them but had reverted to SSM 'to give somebody else a chance' as RSM. The regiment now worked with 17-pounder anti-tank guns fitted on the tough Valentine tank, although the new recruits found the flash of the gun very frightening:

> The range officer put some moving targets up for us. The first one was shot off the rails and we could see the red line of the tracer disappearing through the models and then a whirring ricochet over Bindon Hill and out to sea. Several times small sailing vessels broke the law and sailed within the danger limits and we had to cease firing. It was suggested that a round of 17 pounder across their bows would make them more careful in the future!

The coronation of Queen Elizabeth II gave the Yeomanry a chance of glory in 1953, when, as at previous coronations, each regiment was invited to send a select group to join in the military parades. In the same year the queen approved the presentation to surviving Yeomanry regiments of Dragoon guidons. The 7th Earl Spencer, an embroidery expert, produced the new NY guidon, which was presented to the assembled regiment at Althorp by the Duke of Gloucester, with the long-serving SSM George Jelley being chosen to receive the standard.

Field Marshal the Duke of Gloucester hands the new guidon to SM George Jelley, with Lieutenant Colonel N.P. Foster (right) and Major Sandy Saunders. *(NYA)*

Meanwhile, annual camps continued. The NY changed to armoured cars and 1944 Night March navigator, now Lieutenant Colonel Tom Boardman MC, took command. At Perranporth camp another ex-National Serviceman, 'Tanky' Turner, achieved a victory by error rather than good judgement, not unusual in real battle. His armoured car had got lost at night and he had 'kipped' on Bodmin Moor, before following car tracks in the mud the next day. Putting up an extra aerial, they reported their position. This caused misbelief at HQ, 'You can't be there!':

Just then we saw aerials appearing over the horizon. 'Don't worry' we told control. 'We can see you now'. To which control shouted 'That's not us! That's the enemy! They must not pass. Umpires are on the way'. Sgt Archer and myself devised a plan, with thunder flashes, flares and a Bren gun loaded with blanks. We hid the car and set up an ambush. At that moment two umpires, one of them George Jelley, appeared. The enemy drove up innocently at full speed and we opened fire. There was no doubt about it. The umpires declared the entire 'enemy' troop wiped out. We were the heroes and nobody thought to enquire how we had got lost and why we were away so long (when there was a snug little pub near where we got lost)????

The following year's camp recorded the indestructible George Jelley refereeing the inter-squadron soccer matches at age 63. The NY officers were a little surprised to receive a 'round robin' from a visiting divisional commander, stating tersely that, when coming to camp, 'the GOC does not expect to be fed'. In other words, he was not there to be obsequiously 'wined and dined', as might have happened in other times. He was there to ensure the sharpening up of formation exercises and improvement of individual skills. Increased disciplinary measures could be irksome to some Territorials. Tanky Turner, comedian and mouth organ entertainer of the troops, described an occasion when peacetime spit and polish was exaggerated to a ridiculous degree. The Northampton Drill Hall was having a 'wash and brush up' for a visit by HRH Princess Alice, the Duchess of Gloucester, sister of Lord George Scott:

> There was a very large tiger skin outside the Officers Mess. It was quite old, the beast having been shot in Mysore in 1840. It needed cleaning and the teeth had been lost. The CO thought the Royal Army Dental Corps at Aldershot might help. 'Delighted!' they replied. 'Bring the skin down to our depot'. Some time later I went down to fetch the skin. The Chief Dentist had supervised 'a painless renovation'. Not only had the TEETH been renewed but the nose had been remodelled and the glass EYES highly polished. A wonderful sight for Princess Alice, our Association President. But some of the lads thought it was 'bull gone mad'. And some weeks later somebody stole it, teeth and all!

The mid-1950s and '60s were a time of great perplexity for Yeomanry regiments. There were myriad changes of roles, amalgamations, reductions and even disbandments, so that an entire book might be written about the period. In 1958 the reduced NY became D Squadron of the Inns of Court Regiment, but in 1962 it changed completely in function to 250 (Northamptonshire Yeomanry) Independent Field Squadron, Royal Engineers. In 1956 other amalgamations took place, such as the Scottish Horse and Fife and Forfar Yeomanry eventually becoming the Highland Yeomanry, and one Yeomanry regiment, the North Somersets, found itself merged with an RTR battalion. In 1967 an amalgamation of several county units produced the Royal Yeomanry, one of the four such regiments which would survive into the twenty-first century. Two of the most perplexed counties must have been Leicester and Derby: amalgamated in 1957, in 1967 they were reduced to a cadre, only to find themselves in 1971 a part of the 7th Anglian Infantry Battalion, before they blossomed again as a squadron of the Royal Yeomanry in 1992.

Having moved from 17-pounder Valentines to Ferret and Dingo armoured cars, the Northants had now switched again to learning Royal Engineers' skills such as bridge building. The then Sergeant Bill Hornsey was thrilled to visit the Pied Piper's City of Hamlin where, because of the Cold War, the camping Territorials had to walk out in civilian clothes. Their training consisted of bridging the fast-flowing River Weser:

> At this point the Weser was about 180 to 200 feet wide and needed about 25 pontoons to cross the river. The pontoons were attached to each other with rods and panel pins, each pin weighing roughly 2lbs, hammered home with a sledge hammer. I believe we dropped more pins in the drink than we hammered in. But we achieved the crossing in one day! We then practised manoeuvring a heavy ferry up and down river and for this we had to wear lifejackets. Then back to camp for showers and dinner. Then a two mile walk to a pub, 'The Ice Box'. A small very dark room, sawdust on the floor and

SSM Les Warren parades NY squadron in front of Northampton Drill Hall before a convoy to Wyke Regis camp, 1962. *(Hornsey, NYA)*

a real spittoon, very good beer in ovenware steins with hinged pewter lids. And an ENORMOUS STEAK between two huge slices of bread for 3.50 DM – about 32p!

For the 1962 camp the regiment travelled in convoy from the Drill Hall in Northampton to their annual camp at Wyke Regis in Dorset. It was a formidable convoy consisting of about thirty large vehicles. This included a Ferret scout car, a Humber armoured personnel carrier, a 10-ton Leyland truck, a Commer Tipper, twelve Bedford RL lorries (later known as Green Goddesses and used by the Fire Services), twelve Austin Champs (pre-Land Rover overland vehicles) and other Commer 3-ton lorries.

In the 1960s, in spite of the Russian threat, there was talk of scrapping the TA altogether. A Northampton newspaper reporter went to visit the NY camp at Halton, Lancashire, as part of a campaign using the slogan 'Hands off the TA!' He was invited to a champagne breakfast in the officers' mess but found that TA camps were not all champagne as he was dragged out on a night exercise:

We made our way up the moors where the sappers had been dropped in unknown terrain calling for reliable map-reading. The sappers had to camouflage themselves and try to remain invisible to umpires. As the moon rose the temperature dropped to an unseasonable sub-zero level. From their first rendezvous the Yeomen were to make their way in canoes down three miles of the tortuous river Lune into a fast-flowing torrent. On the rushing river the cold light of dawn revealed a frosty mist which swirled across the banks. As the heavy canoes were man-handled back into three tonners it was easy to see morale was high, even after 15 miles skirmishing. You might expect grumbles from part-time soldiers, but these lads were cheerful enough.

There is talk of scrapping the Terriers. With so many people having so much fun doing such useful service for their country it would certainly be a great pity.[4]

Great pity or not, the Northants lads were to be plunged into a further confusion known as 'suspended animation'. There is a subtle military distinction between suspended animation and disbandment, but in this case it meant that, instead of functioning as a recognisable regiment or squadron, the NY would be transformed into a 'cadre' which, to a civilian's eye, might look like disappearance. In military terms it means a kind of dormant chrysalis, which might one day be revived (particularly in view of the Defence Ministry's 2011 intention to increase the Reserve Forces).

In 1967 a cadre was selected. For a year the NY became A Company, Northamptonshire Regiment, wearing the infantry cap badge but retaining the NY collar dogs, that is to say, double-badged. In 1971 the 7th Battalion of the Royal Anglian Regiment was formed and the cadre was disseminated into this new unit, with bases ranging from Northampton to Grimsby. The cadre of NY luminaries was allocated out: Ralf Martin (red coat toastmaster at annual dinners) becoming CSM of D Company with W.J. 'Bill' Hornsey as his CQMS. Never without his mouth organ, Tanky Turner went on to be CQMS of C Company, and Tanky's CSM Tim Warr was gradually promoted to major. During this process Bill Hornsey received demobilisation papers as 250 Squadron disappeared. He then, on 1 April 1971, had to volunteer again (the first Yeoman to sign on anew) and served another four years. Throughout these changes he retained his own individual army number, 23902758.

Almost simultaneously the NY Association, formed to care for the regiment's veterans, increased in membership as veterans moved towards retirement, with more time to congregate, and as memories became more important. The apparently eternal George Jelley MBE, and later Bill Hornsey, devoted themselves to maintaining the spirit and traditions of the Yeomanry as Hon. Secretaries of the Association. However, at last mortality prevailed: once the longest serving TA soldier, George Jelley was now called to his last parade in the heavens. The NY's last surviving Great War trooper, Alf Dewison died aged 101. Then, at a London Remembrance Service in 1992 there appeared a Boer War Yeoman, George Ives, aged 111, who must qualify for the oldest Yeoman ever. Yet another Yeoman, Major George Jameson MC, won a place in the Guinness Book of Records as Britain's oldest bridegroom, aged 102, and living another five years. What is it about Yeomen?

Meanwhile, as the future of the Yeomanry again became an important parliamentary topic, the 1944 Night March navigator, now Lord Tom Boardman MC, TD, DL, rose to speak in the House of Lords in April 1998, extolling the Yeomanry not only for its prowess in battle but also for its social contribution; quite a change from the antagonistic speeches of members like Mr Hume MP in the 1830s. Lord Tom declared:

In all my time of being connected with the Territorial Army, I cannot recall any instance when, among all the hundreds of people with whom I have served, anyone has done something which had committed him to a civil court. I know of no drug takers, vandals or similar people in the TA … As regards the offences which bog our courts down at the moment, those who had been trained in the Territorial Army have acquired the discipline that goes with it ... They learn on a range of equipment and gain a confidence and maturity which I believe equips them well in whatever role they may take in civil life ... I believe that there is a great role in the TA. It is to supplement the reserve forces, as an aid to the civil power and in the social environment it provides.[5]

In 1998 an event from the 1920s roused strange echoes in the memories of veterans of the NY. The point-to-point trophy which had been misappropriated by the then Prince of Wales suddenly resurfaced in public in circumstances which made it a television news story. On the death of the Duchess of Windsor, the former prince and king's widow, the estate was sold off at public auction. Prominent among the contents was the NY cup, which was bought by a still anonymous Texan oil tycoon for the astonishing sum of $60,000 (plus 15 per cent fees, plus 15 per cent US sales tax), and gained worldwide television coverage. NY's Bill Hornsey appealed through Angela Rippon, the television presenter, for a return of the cup. But, despite its dubious provenance, the Texas purchaser is legally entitled to keep his trophy.

After forty-six years, in 2000 former corporal Percy Sumner in Sheffield had a piece of shrapnel removed from his eye. As he had worked in the steel industry (but in an office) the injury was at first thought to be related to his work. But it proved to be the result of the action in which Rex Jackson won the MM at Loon-op-Zand, where Percy's tank had been hit by a mortar bomb and his face sprayed with shrapnel.

The NY cup awarded annually for the Pytchley point-to-point, won in 1921 by the Prince of Wales, but which he failed to return in 1922. *(NYA)*

Yeomen have made the transition from horses to armoured cars and tanks, and now take to the skies in helicopters. *(c. IWM No Land-02-012-0196)*

In February 2005 there came into force a law which might have had a negative bearing on the incipient Yeomanry if it had been enacted in 1794. Fox hunting, 'as we knew it', was now banned. Huntsmen like the 5th Earl Spencer, the Duke of Beaufort and Lieutenant Colonel Lord Annaly had brought into the infant Yeomanry some of the finest horses to be found anywhere in the world. Now armoured steel leviathans, and indeed helicopters, had replaced the humble equine mount, and the emancipation of the fox had little bearing on military tactics. Of course, the Pytchley and the Beaufort still ride, if somewhat 'foxless'.

The Yeomanry establishment had now been amalgamated, reduced and confirmed as four regiments. On 1 April 1967 the Royal Yeomanry had been formed from former county regiments, each retaining identity and traditions at squadron level. Then in 1971 there were born the Queen's Own Yeomanry, armoured reconnaissance, recruiting from northern England, Northern Ireland and Scotland; the Royal Mercian and Lancastrian Yeomanry with Challenger 2 tanks; and the Royal Wessex Yeomanry in the south-west, in a training role on Challenger 2 tanks. Moving into the twenty-first century, Yeomen were trained in ever more specialist roles and were ready to be posted in and alongside regular troops in active roles overseas.

Some doubt had been expressed about the ability of part-time, annual holiday camp soldiers to be able to cope with modern warfare in its widely varying forms. Experienced soldiers rushed to defend the Terriers, as a certain CSM G.J. Wafer in the 2011 *Daily Telegraph* letters column:

> My TA infantry company is fully manned, with 14 soldiers about to deploy to Afghanistan. They have endured arduous training and have not been found wanting.

They are now fully integrated into platoons in regular battalions and will do the same job – and face the same dangers – as their regular counterparts. Many soldiers in my company have served on operations abroad and some have returned seriously wounded. The TA of today is so far removed from that of [various critics'] experience as to make any comparison meaningless.

So it was that in 2001 the Royal Yeomanry deployed its W Squadron to Kuwait, with the regiment having been trained for a specialist role in NBC (nuclear, biological and chemical war) defence to support other troops. In 2004 men of the regiment paraded in deep snow in Grantham to be briefed about desert war under the blazing sun of Iraq. Their advance guard arrived in Basra on April Fool's Day, but it was serious business ahead. Individual roles varied widely: whilst Lieutenant Charlie Field was 'mentoring the infant Judiciary' in Basra, Sergeant Mark Consadine 'spent many happy hours destroying captured weapons' and Sergeant David Tomlin was creating a personnel database for the local police force which was being rapidly reformed.[6]

Among other specialist roles is that of the Sharpshooters (now Kent and County of London Yeomanry Squadron) who, in December 2009, sent Sergeant Barnard, Corporal Faytaren and Lance Corporal Thompson to Afghanistan during Operation Herrick to fulfil the CORTEZ role 'which is a new intelligence gathering tasking, using the latest camera and sensor technology. It is an exciting role with which the four armoured Yeomanry regiments have been tasked in rotation.'[7]

The Yeomanry regiments also provide valuable service in other fields of activity, such as representing Britain abroad with great aplomb. The NY was once a squadron of the

The FANY (Princess Royal's Volunteer Corps) continue to serve, here practising on the range. *(FANY/PRVC)*

Inns of Courts Regiment, while the Inns of Court themselves have now modulated into the band of the Royal Yeomanry. One of their missions was to the new Hong Kong where they played at a former Royal Naval station, now a Red Army barracks. It seems that the Chinese were fascinated and enchanted, if not with the overall symphonic tones of the band, then with the 'husband and wife' team of percussionists, Graham and Jan Dare, surely a combination never envisaged by William Pitt the Younger.[8]

On a more military note, a regular colonel commanding Yeomen in Afghanistan was in no doubt that CSM Wafer's comments about the Territorials was well founded:

> TA soldiers have proved their commitment to the Army through the sacrifice of enough spare time (weekends and evenings) to cause most Regulars to mutiny on the spot. They have an enthusiasm and commitment to the job that can make us Regulars feel pretty uncomfortable at times. While we are moaning about a tough exercise over a few drinks with a late start on the Monday, the TA soldier will get back late on Sunday, sort out his kit, get ignored by his wife, and get a few hours sleep before another full week of work … I found the TA soldiers I commanded in Afghanistan to be a hugely valuable resource, being friendly and kinetic both within the company and during our various interactions with the local community.[9]

It must be noted also that the Women's Yeomanry, the FANY, continues to thrive. Now renamed the Princess Royal's Volunteer Corps (FANY/PRVC) it has been extended beyond its original nursing service and has become indispensable in emergency communications work, such as terrorist bombings in the UK and during the South Asia Tsunami of 2004 when it did remarkable work in registering missing persons.

Meanwhile, back in Northampton, although Sergeant Reg King, or some modern replacement, no longer needs to mark out bed spaces on the floor to accommodate a sudden mass incursion of recruits, the old Drill Hall continues to resound to the batter of boots, now the footwear of a recovery unit of the Royal Electrical and Mechanical Engineers.

CHAPTER ELEVEN

UNREMITTING REMEMBRANCE
(2012 FOR POSTERITY)

The first return to the graves of long-lost comrades can be awesome but affectionate; eerie but familiar; harrowing but triumphal; provocative but conclusive. There is an aura of expectation that they have been waiting this long, long time for a comrade to come. And the arrival of that comrade brings rest and security at last. There is now some living person present, a comrade, on guard, patrolling, responsible, while they sleep on. Our family: Frank Hickson, George Valentine, Bill Rawlins, Sonny Wellbelove, that unknown Black Watch private …

There is a compelling urge to step quietly through the lush lawns. Not for fear of disturbing them, for they have lain for forty years dreaming who knows what horrors of sudden oblivion and abandonment. But today is for them, as for us, the moment of reunion, recognition, reconciliation. We are again that unique family who understand what is beyond the comprehension of the ordinary person: the shared fears, perils, shedding of blood, whether trivial or fatal; and the enduring debt owed by us, who were fated to soldier on, to those whom the lottery of war selected to receive the bullet, or shard of shrapnel, or disembodied blast. Our being here today, we who so long went absent about our own selfish affairs, resolves all, leaving them, this tiny group together, content.

The psychologist will no doubt argue that those sentiments have no substance; are simply in the mind of the intruder into one of the beautiful sanctuaries maintained by the Commonwealth War Graves Commission. To the returning comrade it is all very real. Yet for the vast majority of Second World War veterans it would be a very long time before such a visit could become viable, or perhaps even desirable.

As at the end of the First World War, demobilised veterans of the 1940s, long-serving original Territorials and younger conscripts, were only too anxious to get back to civilian realities, secure a job, perhaps relocate, get married, start a family, patronise a decent local pub or take up church activities, buy a car, beaver on towards a decent pension. Very few ordinary soldiers could contemplate crossing the English Channel at their own expense, much less be able to explore Normandy or the Arnhem corridor or the Ardennes at leisure. And as to a return to El Alamein, Cassino or Burma, the idea was too remote. For most it would be anything up to forty years before the urge and the means to return would coincide.

Furthermore, the liberated communities, particularly in Normandy, were themselves too devastated to consider welcoming back their unknown liberators. In many villages the front-line troops had passed by without leaving any substantial clues as to their identities. A chance brief encounter with a friendly continental family, such as the farmers who brought flowers to the grave of SSM Sid Turton or Ken Jordan's *hausfrau*, however significant an event in a veteran's memory, did not normally involve an exchange of addresses, much less telephone numbers. And as to hosting and accommodating a large group of visiting veterans, it would be impossible for years to come. In one typical blasted and flamed village, May-sur-Orne, many inhabitants lived in ruined houses for two years before some prefabricated buildings arrived from Sweden. Even then it was eight years before full electricity, gas, drinking water, phone and adequate road facilities had been restored.

The NY Association, like those of other nominally defunct county regiments, had continued to function effectively after the regiment had passed into suspended animation. It had been headed for a while by wartime luminaries such as Lord George Scott and Lord Tom Boardman, and then by post-war Territorials, Peter Symington, Tim Deakin and latterly Ben Howkins, son of the Casablanca colonel. The main purpose was always to support veterans and widows in their physical, material and social needs. At the same time, and although there was no renewing body of active soldiers, diligent honorary secretaries, the late George Jelley and currently Bill Hornsey, organised regular well-attended annual dinners and other anniversary events.

Two such events occurred in 1994 and 1999. The first celebrated both the 200th anniversary of the founding of the regiment and the 50th anniversary of the Normandy campaign. More than a hundred members paraded in front of Althorp House, to the music of a cavalry band, and the salute was taken by the 9th Earl Spencer, Sir John Lowther and Lord George Scott. A similar parade through the streets of Northampton in 1999 preceded the ceremony of laying up the regimental guidon for the last time at the Guildhall. Over the years a number of enthusiasts had researched regimental history, among them Harry Cazenove, A.E. Sandy Saunders and Vic Lawrence. More recently a permanent Yeomanry section has been established at Abingdon Park Museum due to the efforts of Sandy Saunders, Bill Bellamy, Bill Hornsey and Tanky Turner. Much information from individual veterans was distilled through the Annual Report and magazine, with the author as editor since the passing of George Jelley. Another veteran, Wally Wall, printed the magazine for many years.

For forty years veterans of the NY considered themselves to be something of a forgotten or poorly publicised regiment compared with other high-visibility units like the Household Cavalry or the paras. Then in the early 1980s a German research group found the bodies of Major Michael Wittmann and his Tiger crew on the site of the 8 August 1944 battle. This renewed interest in the German tank ace and his nemesis, the humble Yeomen and their Canadian counterparts. The story was first written up for the consumption of the general public in Britain by a freelance writer, once NY trooper, 'Spud' Taylor. A modest spotlight of fame had been turned on the NY.

It was during the late 1970s and early '80s that Second World War veterans of the NY, as with other county and higher formation units, began to think in terms of visiting, as organised groups, their old battlefields and the sacredly maintained cemeteries. These had so far been within the reach of a relatively few individuals and no formal NY Association overseas tour had yet been mooted. At one noisy annual dinner in the

The traditionally uniformed guidon party, Messrs Warren, Hornsey and Turner, march to drumhead service, Althorp bicentenary. *(NYA)*

echoing main hall of the Northampton Drill Hall several members agreed that the time had come to do something about this, and nominated the author to 'do a recce'.

Both in 1944 and latterly, NY veterans had problems in pronouncing Saint-Aignan-de-Cramesnil, causing some to say, 'Why didn't we liberate Bray or Ifs?' Now the author and his wife, Jai, located the village and were given a delighted welcome by the deputy mayor and an especially rapturous welcome by his wife, Monique Bellenger. Monique asked, 'Why have your veterans never returned before? When will they come to see us?' She then produced a tiny barrel, a miniature of the familiar wooden beer barrel, and told their story of gratitude to their unknown liberators.

The entire population of fortified villages had been evacuated in July 1944 and the Bellengers had returned to Saint-Aignan three weeks after the battle. They found houses destroyed, apple orchards devastated, crops burned to ash, burned-out tanks standing on all sides, occasional German bodies still lying in hedgerows and some of their unknown liberators lying in temporary graves around *Le Petit Ravin*. Monique went out into the orchards, gathered some apples from under the shattered trees and then made a special brew of the fortified Calvados of the region. This she stored in the tiny barrel vowing that the tap would never be opened until their liberators could return to drink a liberation toast. The barrel had waited for forty years, its alcoholic strength gradually increasing.

Although an unexpected number of sixty veterans indicated their desire to return to 'Saint-A' on the 40th anniversary of the battle, the community of about a thousand replied in effect 'bring them all', with an offer to accommodate, feed and fete all veterans who could attend an August 1984 event. And join in the celebratory opening of Monique's barrel of panzer-force Calvados. Thus on 8 August some sixty Yeomen, led by the 1944 navigator captain, Tom Boardman, stood on the old battlefield, sharing memories and locating tank positions and other remarkable sites. Such was the success of the visit that there was an immediate demand to return to Holland, to Sint-Michielsgestel, Sint-Oedenrode ('Why didn't we liberate Bray?'), Raamsdonk, the Rhine Crossing and, of course, the Ardennes. Over the next twenty-five years touring parties visited every liberated community from 1944/45 and stood at every NY grave in three countries. Delegations of overseas friends came to Northampton events. Some of those friends will again attend what may be a climactic event in August 2012 when Charles Spencer, 9th Earl, following in the family tradition, welcomes veterans and overseas friends to a special parade and dinner at the home of the original 1794 Troop, Althorp House.

The return visits to Saint-Aignan and elsewhere have had three unanticipated outcomes over the years: a series of memorials dedicated to the regiment; a system of continental remembrance of the regiment's fallen; and a continuing programme of youth education about the realities of war and peace.

Until 1984 there was no mark anywhere of the progress of the regiment from the D-Day beaches to the German border, that is to say, except for the enduring scorched and polluted marks of a Sherman tank's conflagration here and there; the lumps of shrapnel ploughed up by M. Dan and M. Le Baron each year; and the odd Mk IV

Remembrance – the author speaks during the open-air service at NY memorial in Saint-Aignan-de-Cramesnil, 8 August 2004. *(NYA)*

Saint-Aignan-de-Cramesnil memorial to NY erected 2009 after the previous memorial was
desecrated by neo-Fascists. *(NYA)*

mudguard, mess tin or Tiger tank jack discovered by more recent enthusiasts with metal
detectors. Now local people began to mark significant sites. A battle pointer was installed
outside Saint-Aignan and a museum developed. When the pointer was desecrated by
neo-Fascists of the twenty-first century, the local mayor replaced it by commissioning a
fine sculpture of a partially destroyed wall.

A similar wall, honouring the NY and Black Watch, was placed on the battle site at
Sint-Michielsgestel. Outside the Lambertus church in Raamsdonk, local researchers iden-
tified the precise spot where Lieutenant McColl was killed and erected an impressive slab
monument to the young Scot. In the elegant town hall of Vught, where the concentration
camp was liberated, a stained glass window carries the NY badge and also a tribute to the
51st Highland Division as a whole. At La Roche-en-Ardenne, a vital town in the 'Battle
of the Bulge', the council placed a 1944 tank on the main road high above the town to
remember the regiment and the second liberation of the town. At Helden-Panningen in
Limburg the local war memorial also includes a permanent photographic record of the
liberation designed around a portrait of an NY trooper.

Remembrance of another kind issued from a return visit to Zwolle where NY soldiers had joined the rejoicing local inhabitants in the rapturous celebrations of VE Day.
After VE day, and again the following year on the anniversary of VE Day, NY athletes had competed against local athletes in celebration games, cross-country runs, field
events, football, hockey and even chess tournaments. On the first return visit of veterans
in the 1980s, the Dutch second- and third-placed runners of the 1946 cross-country

race appeared, armed with newspaper cuttings of the time, and were delighted to greet the 1946 winner, Trooper Cliff Cuthbertson. Out of this encounter an idea emerged: that this happy sporting relationship ought to be perpetuated as a remembrance event. Again the author was deputed to work out a scheme.

This developed into a standing contact between the NY Association and AVpec 1910, the Zwolle athletic association. A large NY memorial shield, with twenty-five small name shields attached, would be held by AVpec for annual presentation to an outstanding youth athlete of the year, together with an illuminated explanatory scroll. The annual presentation would be a civic occasion to remember the fallen soldiers, both of the regiment and of the Canadians who first entered Zwolle. Such a scheme could extend into posterity.

Continuing until the most recent in 2009, further tours of the veterans awarded similar Youth Remembrance Shields to communities in the three countries. Whilst the Zwolle connection focused logically on athletics, in another town the local mayor and advisors set and judged an annual sixth form essay related to war and peace. In yet another community the award would be for an outstanding youth act or service to the community, and the winner recently was a 7-year-old boy who found his grandmother dead. Using ideas culled from television hospital programmes, he successfully resuscitated the elderly woman and kept her alive until paramedics, called by him, duly arrived. At the presentation it was suggested that, even in eighty years' time, the boy might still be telling his descendants how he won the shield and what the shield was all about: a programme of remembrance unending!

A voluntary group in the area where the boy lived had already undertaken the care of Allied war graves, especially those many who are not interred in the well-regulated official cemeteries. During one of the NY visits the group had the idea of researching the history of a 19-year-old NY soldier killed locally, Trooper Delwyn Price, two of whose crew members (themselves wounded and taken prisoner) accompanied NY tours. The group, VOGW (i.e. War Grave volunteers), led by Marius Heideveld, created a portable display featuring Delwyn to carry to

NY Youth Remembrance Shield, won by outstanding young swimmer Amy van Lier of Kaatsheuvel, Netherlands, 2011. *(VOGW, Waalwijk/NYA)*

local schools whilst teaching about the liberation and why it was so important. Similarly, elsewhere in Holland a schoolmaster, now retired but always most active, Louis Kleijne developed a remembrance programme in local schools, and this is repeated elsewhere. The veterans had involuntarily become a reservoir of information and inspiration for continental organisations concerned to continue remembrance of the fallen and to stimulate the awareness of future generations about issues of war and peace.

Histories of the Second World War, when referring to combat stress, tend to highlight the fact that psychiatric services immediately behind the front line were much more accessible and better equipped than in previous wars. There is also an assumption that the impact of First World War artillery barrages was greater than in the second conflict and therefore caused more shellshock. It is forgotten that some of the 1944/45 barrages, which had to be endured on both sides, were of even greater intensity than in the earlier war and exacerbated by accurate air bombing. And that for those very many of us who did not need immediate psychiatric treatment during the actual battle, but who suffered long-term traumas with which civilian doctors could not cope, there was often no psychiatric provision; checking each 1940s soldier at the busy demob centres would have been an impossible task.

For many veterans the moment of what is now termed 'closure' came with a return to a battlefield site or to the grave of a comrade. On NY tours, as no doubt on many such unit tours to old battlefields, 80-year-old men, toughened by hard-working lives, were not ashamed to break down in tears as the undiagnosed and untreated horrors and nightmares of a lifetime were released and soothed at the foot of a grave. For there lay someone who had shared our travail and then paid a far greater price than we had done.

Although a firm base of amalgamated Yeomanry continues to serve on an area basis, for Northamptonshire and other counties there is no ongoing corpus of active Yeomanry soldiers to carry on traditions. An appeal in the NY magazine by the editor for 'Children of the Regiment' to rally to their fathers' aid brought a response from Melvyn Marchant. His father had been badly burned on 8 August 1944 and promptly discharged from the army with the rather callous judgement 'no longer fulfils the physical requirements for active service'. Melvyn, with wife Maggie, offered to organise a Children of the Regiment group to support Association events. The present Children's chairman, Brian Bower, undertakes the annual task of placing 170 named poppies at the Westminster Remembrance plot each November; Suzanne and Mick Batchelor have become main fundraisers; Caryl Billingham, former Mayor of Brackley, is Hon. Secretary of the Children in their continuing tasks; and the England family produce the magazine.

As the veterans, for whom such associations were formed, pass on, there will be fewer calls on charitable funds. So the double question is raised: is there some useful way in which remaining funds of the association can be utilised (an echo of 1828), and how can we ensure that past sacrifices are not forgotten?

With a successful, perpetual remembrance programme based on youth trophies on the Continent, the NY Association now turned to awarding annual trophies to local groups mainly in the youth sector. However, one variation in this age focus is an award related to a horticultural scheme at the psychiatric hospital for which NY surplus funds purchased the ground in 1828, enabling St Andrew's Hospital, Northampton, to be built. Another trophy reflects the riding and hunting origins of the Yeomanry, in a cup for young disabled riders, and a point-to-point horse race should afford considerable opportunities for media references to the origins of the regiment and the purpose of the trophy programme. The military interests of the association also inevitably lead to several annual awards for proficiency in local cadet branches of the armed forces. Nevertheless, the most poignant if remote places of remembrance are at the 'White Horse' engraved gravestones of the fallen of two world wars.

If at some time or other in the distant past a Yeomanry sword was raised in anger against an unarmed civilian protester, surely any necessary restitution has now been made. The two world wars have seen extreme heroism and considerable sacrifice by Yeomanry soldiers, and that tradition continues. The continuing remembrance of our war dead is not a stagnant, redundant gesture but a contribution to the awareness and security of future generations as they face very different perils.

GLOSSARY

AP	armour-piercing shot
BEF	British Expeditionary Force
Brig	brigadier
Bde	brigade, usually three battalions
Broadsword	(Yeo.) straight sword
Buffalo	armoured amphibious carrier
Capt	captain
Carbine	predecessor of the rifle
CO	commanding officer
Cockade	rosette badge
collar dog	badge worn on lapel/collar
Cornet	the most junior officer (cavalry)
Cpl	corporal
DCM	Distinguished Conduct Medal
D-Day	start day of any battle
DD tank	'swimming tank', waterproofed
Div.	division, usually three brigades
Dragoon	cavalryman trained to fight dismounted
DSO	Distinguished Service Order
Epaulet	shoulder protection – (Yeo) of chain mail
Facings	strips of varied colour material
FANY	First Aid Nursing Yeomanry
Firefly	Sherman tank with larger gun
'Funnies'	tanks adapted for various purposes
Gen.	general
Girth	belly band for saddle
Guidon	small cavalry flag
half-track	vehicle partly wheeled, partly tracked
hands	measurement of horses' height
HE	high-explosive shell
Helmet	rounded protective headgear, often with plumes
Home Guard	part-time defence force

HQ	headquarters
hussar	cavalryman normally wielding sword
lancer	cavalryman with lance as main weapon
L/Cpl	lance corporal, lowest NCO rank
LDV	Local Defence Volunteers (Home Guard)
Lt	lieutenant
Lt Col	lieutenant colonel
Maj.	major
MC	Military Cross
MM	Military Medal
NCO	non-commissioned officer
NY	in this book – Northamptonshire Yeomanry (with apologies to other 'N' Yeomanries)
NYA	NY Association/archives
ORs	other ranks, not officers
Pte	private – lowest military rank
QM	quartermaster
Regt	Regiment – cavalry battalion of several squadrons
REME	Royal Mechanical and Electrical Engineers
RFC	Royal Flying Corps
RSM	regimental sergeant major
RTC	Royal Tank Corps
sabre	slightly curved sword
shako	tall military hat distinct from helmet
SQMS	squadron quartermaster sergeant
sqn	squadron composed of several troops
SSM	squadron sergeant major
Territorial	originally part-time soldier serving only in Britain
Tpr	trooper, lowest cavalry rank (but private also used in cavalry to 1918)
Troop	section of a squadron but also existing as independent units in nineteenth century
TSM	troop sergeant major
VC	Victoria Cross
VE Day	Day of Victory in Europe
WO	warrant officer (SM ranks)
Yeo	Yeomanry – when used with county name is title of a regiment. Also generally all yeomen/regiments

NOTES AND REFERENCES

Chapter One:

1 Retail Price Index comparison charts.
2 All Northamptonshire Yeomanry archive data (NYA) from archives at the Northampton Record Office, or held by the Northamptonshire Yeomanry Association, or in the possession of the author as editor of the NY magazine.
3 Thanks to various Yeomanry museums and regimental records.
4 The Yeomanry Cavalry of Gloucestershire and Monmouth, 1898.
5 Pembrokeshire Museum.
6 National Maritime Museum.
7 As later formulated in Yeomanry Regulations, 1844.

Chapter Two

1 Many contemporary reports and later critiques.
2 Yeomanry Regulations, 1844.
3 The Yeomanry Cavalry of Gloucestershire and Monmouth, 1898.
4 Hansard.
5 1898, *op. cit.*
6 *Household Cavalry in Armour*, 2009.
7 1844, *op. cit.*
8 Lt Col F. Burnaby, Royal Horse Guards, in 1898, *op. cit.*

Chapter Three

1 Arthur Arnold's letters home from NY archives.
2 Lewis, *Yeoman Soldiers.*
3 Glover, *Warfare from Waterloo to Mons.*
4 Capt. Andrew French (Berks Yeo).
5 Arnold, *op. cit.*
6 Lewis, *op. cit.*
7 Glover, *op. cit.*

Chapter Four

1 Spencer family.
2 Dixon, *Memoirs*, NYA.
3 Robson, B., in Holmes, R., *Military History*.
4 Hamilton, Gen. Sir I., 1906 report as GOC.
5 The RGH Hon. Colonel, Maj. Gen. Denaro, still using this long title in 2007, in Lewis, *Yeoman Soldiers*.
6 Spiers, E.M., in Holmes, *op. cit.*
7 Lewis, *op. cit.*
8 Dixon, *op. cit.*
9 Day, *War Diary.*
10 Sassoon, *Memoirs of a Fox-Hunting Man.*
11 Dixon writing later says '56 years ago today'.

Chapter Five

1 All NY references from NY archives.
2 'Brooksby' in *The Field*, Pytchley website.
3 Arriving in 1914 NY men qualified as 'Old Contemptibles'.
4 Rhodes-James, R., in Holmes, *Military History.*
5 Liddell Hart, B.H., *History of the First World War.*
6 The Keep Museum (Dorsets).
7 Internet, *In Memoriam Tpr F.W. Davey.*
8 Lewis, *Yeoman Soldiers.*
9 Neuve-Chapelle quotes from Liddell Hart, *op. cit.*
10 Day, *War Diary.*
11 Knight, diary in NYA.
12 Dixon, *Memoirs*, NYA.
13 Also Tout, *An End of War* re: premonition.
14 Holmes, *Military History.*
15 Liddell Hart, *op. cit.*

Chapter Six

1 Stubbs, NYA.
2 Dixon, *Memoirs*, NYA.
3 Day, *War Diary.*
4 Taylor, B., NYA. Lowther's nose is said to be preserved by family, but not seen by author!
5 Essex Yeo records.
6 Daughter, Joan Simmonds and citation.
7 Lewis, *Yeoman Solders* (water in Sinai).
8 Liddell Hart, B.H., *History of the First World War.*
9 Horse care from various modern sites.
10 Mileham, P.J.R., *The Yeomanry Regiments* and unit sources.
11 Letter home to daughter Margaret, NYA.
12 Author's father, Sapper John Tout, at corps HQ made boots for Earl Cavan, Prince of Wales and NY colonel.
13 New Zealand Ministry for Culture and Heritage.
14 Holmes, *Military History.*

Chapter Seven

1 Jelley, G., *The Years Between*, NYA.
2 See Chapter 10 – NY cup comes to light.
3 George's document *op. cit.* ends with Stockbridge. Much later, as editor of the NY magazine, he encouraged and collected the memoirs of others from two world wars.

Chapter Eight

1 NY archives – to which 'Sandy' Saunders contributed much research in later years.
2 Leary, F., *A Trooper of World War II*, NYA. (Wooton Hall – now the record office where much of the NY information is archived.)
3 Museums and records of various regiments, here and later.
4 Close, *The View from the Turret*.
5 Macksey, K., *Invasion – 1940*.
6 Leary, *op. cit.*
7 As a result Stan became driver of '3 Baker' with the author as gunner. Stan's self-published story, as others quoted, in NYA. And also these and various similar memoirs are in the Second World War Experience Centre (SWWEC).

Chapter Nine

1 Yeomanry Regiments, 1844.
2 2NY war diary and A.E. Saunders.
3 Various memoirs by Moseley, Hicken, Spittles, Leary (all NYA), Thorn and Cloudsley-Thompson also at the Second World War Experience Centre.
4 At the author's tank, acting i.c. Troop Sgt's '3 Able'.
5 Much of the subsequent NY 'travelogue' covered in others of author's books.
6 Ruth Jordan, 2011.

Chapter Ten

1 Various regimental records often accessible from regimental museums.
2 Reversing author's own experience as posted *from* NY *to* KDGs after VE Day.
3 Some anecdotes collected by George Jelley as editor of NY magazine.
4 *Northampton Chronicle & Echo.*
5 Hansard.
6 *Royal Yeomanry Journal*, 2002.
7 *Sharpshooter*, 2010.
8 *Royal Yeomanry Journal*, 2004–06.
9 *Amour*, 2009.

Chapter Eleven

This chapter is based on author's records and personal experience.

BIBLIOGRAPHY

Allen, R.C., *Enclosure and the Yeoman* (OUP, 1992)

Anglesey, Marquess of, *A History of British Cavalry 1826–1929* (Pen & Sword, series)

Bush, M., *The Casualties of Peterloo* (Carnegie, 2005)

Cazenove, H. de L., *Northamptonshire Yeomanry 1794–1964* (NYA, 1966)

Chappell, M., *British Cavalry Equipment, 1800–1941* (Osprey, 1983)

Close, W., *A View from the Turret* (Dell & Bredon, 1998)

Day, C., *War Diary of Sgt Cyril Day, DCM* (NYA, 2011)

Glover, M., *Warfare from Waterloo to Mons* (Cassell, 1980)

Government Department Connected with the Yeomanry, Yeomanry Regulations (1844, also Naval & Military Press, Ltd)

Hastings, M., *Overlord – D-Day and the Battle of Normandy, 1944* (Guild Publishing, 1984)

Holmes. R. (ed.), *The Oxford Companion to Military History* (OUP, 2001)

Judd, D., and Surridge, K., *The Boer War* (Palgrave Macmillan, 2003)

Leary, F., *A Trooper of World War II* (Self/NYA, 2010)

Lewis, J., *Yeoman Soldiers (Gloucestershire 1795–1920)* (Trafford, 2008)

Liddell Hart, B.H., *History of the First World War* (Cassell/Book Club, 1973)

Macksey, K., *Invasion: The Alternate History of the German Invasion of England, July 1940* (Wren's Park, 1980)

Mileham, P.J.R., *The Yeomanry Regiments* (Spellmount, 1985)

Popham, H., *The FANY in Peace and War* (Pen & Sword, 2003)

Sassoon, S., *Memoirs of a Fox-Hunting Man* (Faber & Gwyer, 1928)

Schneid, F.C., *The French Revolutionary and Napoleonic Wars* (Inst. of European History, 2011)

Smith, E.A., *Reform or Revolution* (Sutton, 1992)

'The Yeomanry 1794–1994' in *REGIMENT, The Military Heritage Collection*, special illustrated edition, December 1994/January 1995

Tout, K., *A Fine Night for Tanks* (Sutton, 1998, 2002)

———, *The Bloody Battle for Tilly* (Sutton, 2000, 2002)

———, *By Tank, D to VE Days* (Robert Hale, 1985, 2009)

———, *In the Shadow of Arnhem* (The History Press, 2003, 2009)

———, *Peace in War? War in Peace!* (The Book Guild, 2010)

———, *An End of War* (The History Press, 2011)

Westlake, R., *Territorials 1908–1914* (Naval & Military Press, 2011)

Wyndham Quin, W.H., *The Yeomanry Cavalry of Gloucestershire and Monmouth* (Westley's, 1898; Golden Valley, 2005)

WEBSITES

www.1914-1918.net
www.army.mod.uk/armoured/regiments/1641.aspx (Royal Yeo)
www.army.mod.uk/territorial/24649.aspx (Future Reserves 2020)
www.coghlan.co.uk/territorials.htm
www.historyhome.co.uk/peel/rurallife/swing.htm (riots)
www.militaryhorse.org

INDEX